UNVEILING THE MYSTIC CIPHERS

UNVEILING THE MYSTIC CIPHERS:

Thomas Anson and the
Shepherd's Monument Inscription

Dave Ramsden

Cover photo courtesy of Andrew Baker
Cover design by Cindy Murphy, Bluemoon Graphics
Book design and production by Cindy Murphy, Bluemoon Graphics
Editing by emerson consulting group, inc.

http://www.dave-ramsden.com/

Printed by CreateSpace

ISBN-13:
978-1503119888

ISBN-10:
1503119882

Y·Z·J·F·O·J·R

D·   M·

Acknowledgements

This book would not have been possible without the support of many people. I would specifically like to name a few, beginning with:

My wife and children, who have graciously supported me and put up with my offbeat obsessions over the years.

Andrew Baker, whose thorough research on Thomas Anson and the Shugborough Estate has been invaluable to me and every researcher of the topic over the last thirty years. In addition, his assistance with both the photography and the foreword for the book leave me greatly in his debt.

Many friends, but especially Steve Malloy, Art Flynn, Bill Greene and Ken Munies, all of whom took an interest in the project and gave me feedback on the manuscript or its ideas at various stages.

Experts like Gregory Shaw and David Kahn, who both generously provided direction when I had questions in their areas of expertise. In addition, Bletchley Park's Murlyn Hakon, Oliver Lawn and Sheila Lawn, who provided an early assessment that helped to improve the thesis and the thoroughness of the research.

Tim Hebert, who gave me encouragement and resources. The outstanding staff at Emerson Consulting Group, Ken Lizotte and Elena Petricone, as well as Cindy Murphy of Bluemoon Graphics, whose collective help in editing and preparing the work for publication was invaluable.

And perhaps most importantly, librarians and reference professionals all over the world, from the Lakeville Public Library to Warwick Public Library, Brown University Libraries, University of Pennsylvania Libraries, Oxford's Bodleian Library, the British Museum, the National Archives of London and the Staffordshire Records Office.

TABLE OF CONTENTS

Foreword

FOREWORD

The Shepherd's Monument has looked out from the shade of shrubs and trees for over 250 years. It was always intended to be a mystery to passersby. Those puzzled visitors would have been fairly few for two hundred years. In 1974 the monument was exposed to a wider, mystified, public in Henry Lincoln's BBC documentary "The Priest, the Painter and the Devil." From that point the previously modest folly was swept into a maelstrom of esoteric conjecture, mostly connected with a certain secret society.

I was drawn into this myself. I was already interested in the mythology of Arcadia. I met Henry Lincoln in 1980 and, by chance, I found myself living in a Shugborough estate cottage in 1982. I became a kind of local agent for the authors of *The Holy Blood and the Holy Grail*, organizing a symposium with them in 1983. From then on research was shared and though my links with Shugborough and Staffordshire libraries I was passed many theories about the monument and its cipher.

The storm of usually incoherent and mad ideas completely obscured any serious research. In recent years it has died down. It won't go away — but the *Prieuré de Sion* has withered and revealed itself as a joke by an eccentric occultist and an alcoholic comic actor. (Look up Philippe de Chérisey on imdb.)

But was it a serious joke? A ludibrium? So much genuine mystery was swept up in the whirlwind. And the monument remains. It is a gate into mysteries. We may never know how much depth of mystery was intended by Thomas Anson but as time goes by he emerges as a fascinating figure. Anything could be possible.

Dave Ramsden has looked into the shadow with a clear eye. He has found intriguing material that leads us into a forgotten world of ideas. It's time to take the Shepherdess's invitation into mystery seriously.

Andrew Baker
District Manager, Stafford, Staffordshire Libraries and Arts

Preface

PREFACE

In 1967 David Kahn wrote the first exhaustive history of cryptography, beginning with its earliest appearance thousands of years ago in Egypt and following its progress throughout history until modern times. In his examination of early cryptography, Kahn pointed out that the first recorded form of encryption was found in hieroglyphics on Egyptian tombs. The Egyptians were the

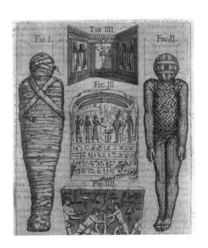

Figure 1: Egyptian funerary practices, from Athanasius Kircher's *Oedipus Aegyptachus*.

first known authors to actively try to transform the writing from a basic sign, whose meaning was easily translated, into a more complex sign whose translation required more involvement on the part of the reader.

Why? Because this transformation added a second level of meaning to the text. The first was the standard, or plaintext meaning of the language. The second, deeper significance was the effect gained by using some means to alter the presentation of the text to the reader. A simpler, more straightforward symbol or word could have been used, but the author chose a more unique symbol to add a greater sense of dignity to the tomb, or to catch the eye of more readers. Eventually this led to what modern culture might see as word-games, which both challenged the reader and entertained them at the same time. Kahn states:

> As Egyptian civilization waxed... these transformations grew more complicated, more contrived and more common...
>
> ...But many inscriptions are tinctured, for the first time, with the second essential for cryptology – secrecy. In a few cases, the secrecy was intended to increase the mystery, and hence the arcane magical powers of certain religious texts. But the secrecy in many more cases resulted from the understandable desire of the Egyptians to have passerby read their epitaphs and so confer upon the departed the blessings written therein. They introduced the cryptographic signs to catch the reader's eye, make him wonder, and tempt him into unriddling them – and so into reading the blessings.[1]

From cryptography's inception in antiquity through its development over time; from the middle-ages to the renaissance and the modern era, it has been inextricably connected to the intertwined worlds of religion, science and the occult. Language contains an elemental power. Secret language exponentially expands the perception of that power. It is not an accident that the publications of many of the greatest innovators in cryptography, such as Johannes Trithemius and Blaise de Vigenère, often delve just as deeply into esoteric studies of religion, alchemy and occult knowledge as they do into the art of encryption. Perhaps this is the reason why the mystery of secret writing, whether on an ancient tomb or in a Sherlock Holmes novel, creates an intoxicating lure for the curious mind.

In the modern era this connection has lessened somewhat, especially as technology has accelerated the capabilities and prevalence of cryptography in every aspect of daily life. Specialists in the area are now mathematicians and engineers, not historians, clerics and alchemists. The mystery has faded. The mixtures of disciplines have separated. Now they present themselves as independent fields of study, neatly arranged on different pages of our college course catalogs. Some have disappeared altogether. And cryptography is now a commodity to be purchased on the common market and deployed by the masses, with little or no understanding of its functional workings or the context of its development.

Much of the early fascination of cryptographic mysteries is gone, but some esoteric puzzles still remain. The Shepherd's Monument is one of them. It crosses the timeline of cryptographic history at that point just as the magic was fading, as science began to ascend to the throne of knowledge and divorce itself from other less tangible fields. Here, an English gentleman at the crossroads of the Rosicrucian Enlightenment and the scientific revolution set in stone a marble picture and ten cryptic letters. At this unique moment in time, Thomas Anson built a monument that holds a secret. A Shepherdess's Tomb whose inscription, like those Egyptian tombs thousands of years before it, begs us to spend some time working out its ciphers. They catch our eye, make us wonder, and tempt us to unriddle them – and so perhaps, into reading their blessings.

---

[1] Kahn, David. *The Code Breakers: The Comprehensive History of Secret Communication from Ancient Times to the Internet*, (New York: Scribner, 1996), 71-72.

Thomas Anson

Thomas Anson & the Shepherd's Monument

During late March of 1773, a quiet but well-connected English gentleman retired to his townhouse in fashionable St. James Square, London. Thomas Anson, always a devoted patron of the arts, now hired a harpist to comfort him in what were destined to be his final hours.

In his lifetime Anson had socialized with some of England's most brilliant personalities. He served in parliament, belonged to numerous clubs and organizations, and over time had grown to be one of the wealthiest men in England; largely due to the fortune left to him by his brother, the celebrated Admiral George Anson. As

Figure 2: Portrait believed to be Thomas Anson, dressed in Eastern attire. This was probably painted upon his return from the Grand Tour. ©National Trust Images.

a young man Thomas Anson had been on the Grand Tour of Europe, and throughout his life he travelled extensively through Europe and the Eastern Mediterranean region then known as the Levant. From Greece southeast through today's Syria and Egypt, Anson travelled the near east and became fascinated with its culture.

Through their family, both Anson brothers had developed relationships with many other influential members of English society. Their uncle, Thomas Parker, the 1st Earl of Macclesfield, was the last non-royalty to rule England as Regent. Through Parker, the Ansons met many influential figures, such as Richard Mead, renowned doctor, philanthropist, bibliophile and physician to the king. Sir Isaac Newton was also well known to the family, with Thomas Parker serving as one of Newton's pallbearers at his state funeral. The family tutor was William Jones Sr., a mathematician

Figure 3: Close up view of the marble bas relief and inscription tablet. Courtesy of Andrew Baker.

who coined the symbol for *pi* and was a close associate of Newton. Jones himself eventually proposed Thomas Anson into membership at the Royal Society. Throughout his life Anson moved amongst the wealthy and influential, from nobles to intellectuals, politicians, and artists.

Today however, Thomas Anson is perhaps best remembered for the massive renovation of his family estate at Shugborough Hall in Staffordshire. On the estate, which is owned by the National

Trust and open to the public, are some of the earliest examples of Greek revival architecture in England. No doubt inspired by Anson's early travels, many of the monuments and buildings are also based upon James "Athenian" Stuart and Nicholas Revett's drawings, which appeared in their groundbreaking 1762 publication, *The Antiquities of Athens.* Anson was a member of the Dilettante Society, which had funded the pair's expedition to Greece, and he leveraged these connections to engage Stuart on a number of the works.

Anson had purchased much of the neighboring land and proceeded to create a private, pastoral Arcadia in the midst of the English countryside. Working with designers like Stuart and Thomas Wright, he filled the fields and gardens with monuments and artwork that re-created not only the glories of classical Greek architecture, but a diverse selection of works inspired by ancient Greek, Roman, Chinese, and Druidic cultures. Walking the estate today one will find monuments such as a Doric Temple, a Chinese House, the Lanthorne of Demosthenes, the Temple of the Winds, a Druidic Ruin, Triumphal Arch, and more. No piece of the eclectic collection, however, has attracted so much curiosity and speculation as that known as the Shepherd's Monument.

That is because, with Thomas Anson's departure, posterity inherited a mysterious, ten-letter cipher whose elusive solution appears to have passed from this world to the next with its creator. Those ten letters have survived for some 250 years, etched into the marble of the Shepherd's Monument, never explained satisfactorily by the speculation and stories that have been associated with it. The monument, set back amongst shrubs on the banks of the modest River Sow close to its confluence with the River Trent, is one of many marvelous and unique forms of architecture which adorn the estate. It is perhaps the most enigmatic, however, for the mystery of its cryptic letters and the rather esoteric nature of its design.

Figure 4: Nicholas Poussin's *Les Bergers d'Arcadie*

The monument consists of a rustic stone archway that has the appearance of a grotto, itself enclosed within stylized pillars and a stone entablature. Within the rustic arch are set two marble tablets, which are the work of the prominent sculptor Peter Scheemakers. The upper tablet contains a frieze of the famous Nicholas Poussin painting, *Les Bergers d'Arcadie* or *The Shepherds of Arcadia*. The dimensions of the sculpture have been modified to make the tablet much narrower than the original painting. In addition, a number of unique elements have curiously been added to the scene on the frieze, such as the image of a sepulcher and a small pyramid. Moreover, the marble has been sculpted depicting a reverse image of the original painting. Below the Poussin frieze is the second marble tablet, which contains the mysterious inscription: eight letters separated by seven punctums, and below them two broadly spaced letters, each with a punctum of their own:

O·U·O·S·V·A·V·V

D·   M·

Evidence left by Thomas Anson's contemporaries indicates that the letters compose a "mystic cipher" that conceals the Shepherdess's name.[2] Moreover, the 18th century travel writer Thomas Pennant recorded that the monument held a unique personal significance for Anson, stating both that Anson directed its creation and that "he was wont often to hang over it in affectionate and firm meditation."[3] In an 1817 publication, *A Topographical and Historical Description of the Parish of Tixhall*, the authors quote Pennant's description of the monument, but in a footnote point out that Pennant neglected to mention the cipher, adding, "The meaning of these letters Mr. Anson would never explain and they still remain an enigma to posterity."[4]

This book proposes a hypothesis to explain both the mystery of those letters and the design of the monument they are inscribed upon. The first half of the book focuses on the examination of the technical details of the monument and the inscription, as well as the other historical evidence left to us by the Ansons and their contemporaries. It includes a close reading of the written references to the monument, examination of the context within which the monument's symbolism works, and a methodical technical decryption of the cipher, aided by the historical evidence presented. The second half of the book attempts to better understand the meaning conveyed by both the cipher and the monument, by beginning to understand the ideas taking root amongst Thomas Anson and his peers. These ideas are spiritual and philosophical at their core, rooted in syncretism and possessing strong ties to the forms of western mysticism expressed by Christian Kabbalists and hermetic scholars. This book does not, however, presume to be indisputable; nor does it claim to fully express all of the levels of meaning that the mystery may carry. Nevertheless, it does propose a potential solution that bears both consideration and further in-depth study.

---

[2] Anonymous Poem of 1767, Records of the Anson Family of Shugborough, Earls of Lichfield, Staffordshire Hall of Records.

[3] Thomas Pennant, *The Journey from Chester to London* (London: B. White, 1782), 93.

[4] Clifford, *A Topographical and Historical Description of the Parish of Tixhall in the County of Stafford* (Paris, 1817), 65.

PART ONE

Decrypting the Shepherd's Monument Inscription

THE TOMB IN THE GARDEN

The first question one must answer while examining the Shepherd's Monument is this: what exactly is it? The design is so unique that one may wonder what its purpose is. The answer, which must be established before proceeding into its deeper mysteries, is confirmed by examining the historical evidence available to us. Most modern day sources refer to the subject of our study as the Shepherd's Monument. However, unpublished manuscripts from associates of the Ansons refer to it as the "Shepherdesses Tomb" (sic). This is evidenced in an anonymous poem written by an associate of the Ansons and presented to Thomas Anson in 1767. The poem, now held in the Staffordshire Records Office, states:

> ...*Observe you rising hillock's form,*
> *Whose verdant top the spiry cypress crowns,*
> *And the dim ilex spreads her dusky arms*
> *To shade th'ARCADIAN Shepherdesses tomb...*[5]

Figure 5: The Shepherd's Monument in the gardens at Shugborough estate. Courtesy of Andrew Baker

These lines identify the work not as the Shepherd's Monument, but as the "Arcadian Shepherdesses Tomb." Supporting this interpretation is the period interpretation of the Poussin painting, which is replicated in marble on the monument. Within the Anson library was a work by Abbe Jean Baptiste Du Bos, entitled Critical Reflections on Poetry, Painting and Music.[6] Du Bos was a member and secretary of the French Academy. In this work Du Bos makes specific reference to the Arcadia painting by Poussin, describing it as a funerary monument dedicated to a young Arcadian maid. [7]

The lines of the poem above also describe the environs of the tomb, specifically noting the two types of trees which adorn the plot. Shading the monument is the ilex, or holly, which is associated with death and rebirth. Atop the hill is the cypress, which is symbolically associated with funeral pyres, mourning and tombs. This association is expressed by classical authors such as Ovid and Vergil. Ovid wrote: "A funeral altar suits me, ringed with cypress which belongs to the dead."[8] Vergil related the same connection in the Aeneid, writing, "Altars are erected for the shades, gloomy with black ribbons and dark cypress."[9]

The unknown author of the Shugborough poem fills each line with descriptions that carry the very real symbolic nature of the artwork and its setting, clearly portraying the work to be a funerary altar erected to honor the Shepherdess's shade. However, it is not the only record left to us that demonstrates that the Anson's contemporaries understood the sculpture to be a tomb. A similar description is also used in the short 1772 poem by the Ansons' friend, Sir William Bagot of Blithfield:

> O could you see how Nature pours,
> Profuse her verdure and her flowers,
> Her earliest, freshest bloom,
> Embroidering all the hallow'd ground,
> With blue-bells, daisies, violets, round
> Your Shepherdesses Tomb.[10]

This phrasing is a significant point, as it continues to support the idea that the founding design for the piece is exactly what the phrasing clearly states: a tomb, or more specifically, a Greco-Roman funerary altar. By identifying the piece as a tomb, and by characterizing the ground surrounding the tomb as "hallow'd", Bagot introduces the concept of veneration, most commonly understood as the act of honoring an icon or relic through ritual devotion.

The poetic testimony of Anson's contemporaries is a very clear indicator of the monument's role. Not only do both sources specifically refer to it as a tomb, or more specifically the "Shepherdesses tomb", they also build upon this theme by referencing aspects of the landscape, such as the ilex and cypress trees, which signify its role as a memorial. The design of the artwork on the Shugborough estate was not haphazard. Thomas Anson and his commissioned artists were pioneers in the study of classical architecture, and were equally versed in classical mythology and the language of symbolism. It is reasonable to argue that the choices they made in landscaping and designing the gardens were intended to complement the thematic elements of the monument itself. But, in order to understand the design of the funerary altar and its role as a vital part of classical life and art, it is important to briefly examine the concept of the memorial during this period.

In classical society, it was believed that a person who did not receive a proper burial would wander the afterlife in unrest. Thus, proper memorials were an important part of Greco-Roman culture, to the point that they eventually evolved into ancestor worship and the cult of the dead. The concept, clearly tied to mortal hopes and fears regarding the next world, placed a heavy duty upon ancestors to ensure their dead were buried and memorialized. This duty was so important that even if a body were unrecovered, a Cenotaph would be erected as a monument to the spirit of the departed.[11]

In these monuments it was imperative that the memory of the deceased be preserved, and thus pictorial commemorations became common elements of the funerary stele. These steles took the form of an upright, rectangular stone bearing the image of the deceased. The image idealized the subject in life, usually in a domestic context that would signify their occupation. The image was accompanied, as well, by an inscription denoting their name, and at times, a dedication. The entire monument would typically be enclosed in an architectural edifice, which framed the work. In describing these free-standing stelae, J. M. C. Toynbee writes:

> More elaborate are the stones on which the text is confined to a die or panel specially reserved for it, while the field or fields above or below it, or both above and below, are occupied by figure scenes showing the deceased fighting on horseback or hunting or reclining at the funerary meal, or presenting some other group or episode or a set of objects appropriate to his career. Here the picture element very often dominates the epigraphical.[12]

At its most basic level, this is the exact design of the Shepherdess's tomb. The central marble edifice is divided into two parts. The lower portion is the inscription die, bearing the name (encrypted), along with the dedication, "D.M." The upper section is the frieze depicting the deceased in life. The scene captured on the frieze properly depicts the Shepherdess in life, identifying her role and revealing her connection to the tomb of another.

The poems written by the Ansons' contemporaries used the terminology they did because it was clear to these individuals that the monument was a tomb. If not an actual tomb, a memorial Cenotaph created in the Greco-Roman style. In design, it bears symbolism that immediately sets it apart as a funerary monument. Moreover, the visual layout of the monument, from its size and shape to the placement of the carved relief of its subjects, as well as the inscription below, all follow the classic design of a Greco-Roman sepulcher. The ciphertext that conceals the name certainly confuses the recognition of the inscription as a name, but once this mystery is revealed the memorial's form and function are shown to naturally complement one another. We take the first step towards recognizing these connections next, as we begin to examine the inscription below the relief.

THE SACRED INSCRIPTION

Before beginning to decipher the eight central letters of the Shugborough inscription, the D. and the M. at either far end of the text are analyzed independently. This step is the simplest aspect of the process, and it serves to reinforce the hypothesis we have put forth thus far: that the monument represents a tomb.

Figure 6: Close up view of the inscription tablet. Courtesy of Andrew Baker

The lower visual placement of the letters, as well as their situation at the extreme left and right of the central inscription, leads the decoder to remove them and evaluate them on their own. As indicated by previous researchers, they represent the Latin phrase *Dis Manibus*. The inscription D. M. is quite common on Roman tombstones and is translated as a dedication "to the Manes [of]", followed by the name of the person being memorialized. Another variation of this inscription is D.M.S., or *Dis Manibus Sacrum*, which translates as "sacred to the Manes [of]." Here the Manes represented the souls of the dead, worshipped as gods. In her work, *Death and Burial in the Roman World*, J. M. C. Toynbee discusses the inscription:

> In Homer and in classical Greek literature and art the dead in the underworld, if condemned to a shadowy and tenuous condition, as contrasted with the fullness of human life on earth, retained their names and were still to some degree themselves. Of this belief in the survival beyond the grave or a person's identity the earliest known evidence in Rome dates from the first century BC, when Cicero, Livy and Virgil use Manes of the souls of individuals; while from the Augustan age onwards tomb inscriptions combine the traditional formula of collectivity, *D(is) M(anibus)* or *D(is) M(anibus) S(acrum)*, with the personal name or names of the deceased in the nominative, genitive or dative case.

Thus, the recognition of D.M. as a common epitaph on the stone memorials of the Romans throughout Europe is consistent with the architectural design of the monument, leading one even closer to the recognition of the memorial as a funerary altar. It also leads the decoder to consider the remainder of the inscription, the eight letters above, as representative of the name of the deceased. This is necessary, because the name is not only the common inscription which accompanies these initials, but the name is also (quite logically) required to grammatically complete the memorial phrase.

THE SACRED NAME

As we have indicated, the eight central letters of the inscription represent the name of the person to whom this stone is a memorial, disguised through the use of ciphers. In addition to the use of the epitaph, Dis Manibus, and the implication that the letters above this dedication must represent a name, there is an additional hint which points towards this conclusion. It lies in the Staffordshire Records Office, among the Anson papers.

Within the care of the Staffordshire Records Office is the long, anonymous poem regarding the Shugborough estate, which we have previously referenced. The poem, which is dated July 7, 1767, provides a lyrical inventory of the artwork that decorates the grounds. It is understood to be an anonymous gift of poetry, presented to Thomas Anson by an associate who earnestly wished his or her identity to be kept secret. (It is sometimes ascribed to Anna Seward, but this is due to confusion with a quite different poem in the Staffordshire Archives. The Miltonic style is very different from any of her works.) Of the many lines of verse, the complete section which describes the Shepherd's Monument is as follows:

> ...Observe you rising hillock's form,
> Whose verdant top the spiry cypress crowns,
> And the dim ilex spreads her dusky arms
> To shade th'ARCADIAN Shepherdesses tomb:
> Of PARIAN stone the pile: of modern hands
> The work, but emulous of ancient praise.
> **Let not the Muse inquisitive presume**
> **With rash interpretation to disclose**
> **The mystic ciphers that conceal her name.**
> Whate'er her country, or however call'd
> Peace to her gentle shade. The Muse shall oft
> Frequent her honour'd shrine, with solemn song
> Gives respite from the long days weary task,
> And dewy HESPER brightens in the west,
> Here shall the constant hind, & plighted maid
> Meet, & exchange their tokens, & their vows
> Of faith, & love. Here weeping Spring shall shed
> Her first pale snowdrops, bluebells, violets,
> And Summer's earliest roses blossom here...14

This poem, as we have already observed, reveals a great deal about the monument and the Shepherdess. In addition to identifying the monument as a tomb, the lines contain more clues for our investigation. Of great significance is the phrase "Let not the Muse inquisitive presume / With rash interpretation to disclose / The mystic ciphers that conceal her name." This text accomplishes several things. It confirms the fact that the shrine is dedicated to a woman, represented by the Shepherdess. It also very clearly indicates that the inscription represents the woman's name, hidden through the use of ciphers.

Subtly, though, the poem does even more. First, the poem exhibits a devotional tone. It does this by using laudatory phrasing, such as 'emulous of ancient praise', 'honour'd shrine' and 'solemn song.' This tone subsequently imbues upon the Shepherdess a divine persona. Furthermore, when the author states, "whate'er her country, or however call'd", he or she draws reference to the syncretic tradition of the mother-goddess, called by many names in many countries, but united as one feminine deity. And the allusion to the syncretic tradition cements the concept of the Shepherdess as representative of a feminine goddess type, with similar traits across cultures, though her name may be different in each.

Syncretism is basically the combination of similar traits found in the religious practices of different cultures. For example, both Roman and Greek cultures had a king of the gods who ruled in the sky and wielded a lightning bolt. In Greece, his name was Zeus. In Rome, his name was Jupiter. Both figures had sacred names within their cultures, but both had very similar traits. Over time, as the cultures integrated, both names were understood to signify the same divine entity.

The syncretic phrasing in the Shugborough poem parallels one of the best-known historical records of this tradition. It lies in one of the second century writings of Apuleius, himself a priest who had been initiated into several mystery schools. The writing is titled *The Metamorphosis*, and it is through this work that scholars have gained much of their knowledge of the Egyptian mystery cult of Isis. Anson possessed a copy in his library at Shugborough,[15] and as a member of the Egyptian Society as well as the man who commissioned a frieze of Isis on the ceiling of his dining room, Anson would have certainly been familiar with the tale. The climactic passage which is often quoted by scholars to demonstrate the ancient understanding of syncretism appears in Chapter 11 of the tale, when the protagonist, Lucius, passionately invokes the goddess Isis in a theurgic ritual:

> "O Queen of Heaven!, Be thou Ceres, *alma mater*, genesis of grain, you who were overjoyed at the recovery of your daughter... or be thou celestial Venus, who gave birth to Love and so wove the heterogeneity of the sexes into the web of the world's beginning... or be thou Diana, sister of Phoebus Apollo, who relieve and revive pregnant women in the pains of their labor by your relaxing restoratives...or be thou blood-curdling Proserpina...by whatever name, with whatever rite, in whatever face it is fitting to call upon you, be thou now my bulwark against tribulations..."[16]

If we compare this to the anonymous poem given to Anson by one of his peers, it is easy to see the similarities in phrasing between the two, indicating a clear allusion in the modern poem to the work by Apuleius.

The author of the 1767 poem was certainly aware of syncretism. A footnote discusses a statue of Adonis:

> "Adonis, Thammuz, & Osiris, are Greek, Phenician & Egyptian names for the same person."[17]

The Shepherd's Monument then, as understood by Anson's peers, clearly functions within the same syncretic tradition that Apuleius communicated thousands of years earlier. Whatever the country, and whatever she may be called there; be it Ceres, Venus, Diana, Proserpina, Hekate or Isis, she is understood to be one single divine being. While the eight-letter inscription may not bear the name of Isis, it is clear that the Shepherdess is a spiritual type, representative of the same ancient goddess figure. The deeper secret lies in the name used to identify her, and in Thomas Anson's motivation for keeping it a mystery.

We will examine the syncretic tradition in more detail later in this work, because it lies at the very heart of the design of the monument, and of the Shugborough estate in general. For the moment, however, the key thing we will take away from the poem's syncretic phrasing is the idea that the Shepherdess possesses a divine persona, and as such her name itself is a sacred thing.

In the tradition of sacred names, it is common for a divine name to be held so sacred that it may not be uttered. For male divinities, the Hebrew Tetragrammaton is perhaps the best-known example of this concept. This four-letter symbol, sometimes written with hyphens to denote the presence of three vowels in-between, is often represented as such: YHWH, or in Hebrew יהוה. The identity of the vowels and the correct pronunciation of the name was known only to the high priest and was so closely guarded that it was ultimately lost in 70 AD when the Romans obliterated the center of Hebrew worship by destroying Herod's Temple in Jerusalem. The esoteric nature of this knowledge has caused the concept to take on a mythic nature in some western mystery traditions, such as the Kabbalah and speculative freemasonry. The quest for the lost word has become a metaphor for the quest for the ideal, knowledge of God, or mystic gnosis itself.

Divine feminine names were also revered by their worshipers. Pausanias, the 2nd century Greek geographer, published a travel guide to Greece which was known to all explorers of region during Anson's time (indeed, a copy of the work was in the Shugborough library).[18] In it he describes a Greek mystery cult devoted to a goddess whose name was held so sacred by followers that it was forbidden to be uttered.[19] Like the Tetragrammaton, it has now been lost forever. Only those initiated into her cult knew her true name, and outside of the cult she could only be referred to as "Despoina" or "Lady." Other mystery schools in Greece might have several worship centers for their cult, but in this one case, similar to the Hebrew faith, there was only one true center for worship. It was in Arcadia, in the city of Lykosoura. With that knowledge, it is more than a little interesting to remember the words that the Shepherdess contemplates: ET IN ARCADIA EGO. Even in Arcadia, I am.

Figure 7: Close up of the mysterious Latin phrase ET IN ARCADIA EGO, inscribed on the sarcophagus. Courtesy of Andrew Baker.

The inscription hides a name, and that name belongs to the Shepherdess. Moreover, the name is regarded as having sacred properties. Nevertheless, the tradition of syncretism demonstrates the use of many names for the same goddess. Thus, one must wonder what the significance of this one, hidden name may be. In order to understand the answer, we must examine the ciphers used in the inscription of the name.

Madame d'Urfé's
Mystic Ciphers

There has been a close relationship between ciphers and mysticism ever since the first Egyptian scribe began experimenting with phrases on sacred tombs. From the Hebrew tradition of Kabbalah, to renaissance abbot Johannes Trithemius who purportedly used spirits to transmit concealed knowledge, as well as early doctors and chemists who used codes and symbols to conceal the secrets of alchemy, western mysticism and the art of concealing knowledge have always walked similar paths.

One story from Anson's time illustrates this idea well. Across the English Channel, in the bustling city of Paris, the nobility of France were as intrigued as the rest of Europe by the growing fashion for the free exchange of ideas. Moreover, many shared a penchant for the mysterious, fascinated with the spread of secret societies and esoteric traditions. They hosted parties and invited charismatic and eccentric personalities, such as the androgynous French spy Chevalier d'Eon, Italian adventurer and occultist

Alessandro Cagliostro, and the enigmatic Comte de Saint Germain, all of whom lived shadowy lives between the tangible courts of the elite and the legends of the esoteric underworld.

One Parisian noblewoman, Jeanne Camus de Ponecarré, marquise d'Urfé, was as noted for her devotion to the occult as she was for her high position in society. After the loss of her husband and the death or estrangement of all of her children, she spent much of her time engrossed in the study of magic and alchemy, seeking the secrets of the alchemists' *magnum opus*. She had great wealth, and had inherited a vast library full of works on magic, alchemy, and science, that no doubt included many of the volumes the Earl of Macclesfield held in his massive collection at Shirburn Castle.

Altera nunc rerum facies,me quero,nec adsum
Non sum qui fueram,non puto esse: fui.

At one stage of her life, Mme. d'Urfé met a charming and mysterious Italian named Giacomo Casanova, the famed lover, confidence man and adventurer, who earned her good graces and ultimately her patronage. This was done in part through his ability to play upon her fascination with esoteric knowledge. In his autobiography, Casanova tells of a story in which we see the close connection between ciphers and mysticism.

Figure 8: Giacomo Casanova, from the frontispiece of his 1788 novel *Icosameron*

He tells us of his first visit to Mme. d'Urfé's estate, the dinner they had and some polite conversation afterwards in which the two began to get to know one another. It did not take long for the topic of conversation to turn to his host's passion for learning, especially esoteric subjects. Casanova tells us that, "After the dessert ... Madame d'Urfé began to discuss alchemy and magic, and all the other branches of her beloved science, or rather infatuation." Upon discussing the various stages of the Great Work of Alchemy, Casanova learned that Mme. d'Urfé believed herself to possess a manuscript that described the secret process of transmuting lead to gold. He states, "She then shewed me a collection of books that had belonged to the great d'Urfé, and Renee of Savoy, his wife; but she had added to it manuscripts which had cost her more than a hundred thousand francs. ... She shewed me a short manuscript in French, where the Great Work was clearly explained. She told me that she did not keep it under lock and key, because it was written in a cypher, the secret of which was known only to herself."[20]

The noblewoman gave a copy of the manuscript to Casanova as a challenge, believing that he could not decipher it. But weeks later, he surprised her by stating that he had read the enciphered text, coyly adding that it contained nothing he did not already know. As proof, he revealed to her the key she had used to encipher the text. To which Mme. d'Urfé responded, "This is too amazing, I thought myself the sole possessor of that mysterious word — for I had never written it down, laying it up in my memory — and I am sure I have never told anyone of it."[21]

In closing his tale, Casanova relates the still-close connection between people's understanding of ciphers and the occult, stating that, "I might have informed her that the calculation which enabled me to decipher the manuscript furnished me also with the key, but the whim took me to tell her that a spirit had revealed it to me. This foolish tale completed my mastery over this truly learned and sensible woman on everything but her hobby. This false confidence gave me an immense ascendancy over Madame d'Urfé, and I often abused my power over her."[22]

We might write off this tale as a wild embellishment told in order to make the memoirs more interesting, and to make Casanova appear to be more of a genius. But, we do possess evidence that Casanova was, in fact, well versed in the use of polyalphabetic substitution ciphers such as the one he describes. In fact, on a letter he wrote in 1791 exists a short enciphered text using the same cipher and the exact same key which Mme. d'Urfé zealously kept secret, the word "Nebucadnezzar."[23] We cannot prove that he mathematically cracked her cipher, as he states (indeed, no record exists of a polyalphabetic cipher being broken by anyone until the next century), but a confidence man such as himself may have found other ways to reveal its secrets.

What we can take away from this story, however, is the fact that ciphers and esoteric fields of study went hand in hand during this period in history. In addition, the polyalphabetic substitution cipher appears to have been used often enough in such matters to have been relatively common among members of learned society. And finally, Casanova makes a point we will refer to in our decryption of the Shugborough cipher, which is that the cipher is basically a mathematical relationship between three variables: the cleartext, the ciphertext and the key. Once one knows the values of any two of these elements, it is quite possible to calculate the third.

THE SHEPHERDESS'S
MYSTIC CIPHER

This solution contends that the primary cipher that encrypts the Shepherdess's name is a polyalphabetic substitution cipher, just like that which Casanova and Mme. d'Urfé used during the same period. The concept of the polyalphabetic cipher was first introduced in the 15th century by Leon Battista Alberti. Improved upon by Johannes Trithemius and Giovan Battista Bellaso in the 16th century, it is today perhaps best known as the Vigenère cipher, for the French mathematician Blaise de Vigenère, whose subsequent publications on it achieved more popular attention. The version used for the Shugborough cipher appears to be a one introduced by Giovanni Sestri in 1710. A version similar to Sestri's was later popularized by Sir Charles Beaufort in the 19th century and is often known as the Beaufort cipher.

A substitution cipher is a cipher that substitutes the letters of the alphabet in the original message, or cleartext, with a different alphabet, creating the ciphertext. For example, the letter A might be replaced with the letter B, B with C, and so on. However, in a polyalphabetic substitution cipher, multiple alphabets are used to encrypt the message. This makes cracking the cipher more difficult. To decipher the message, one must know how many substitute alphabets were used and which alphabets they were. A key was used to define the number of alphabets and the letter they began with. A thirteen-letter key such as Madame d'Urfé's "Nebucadnezzar" would mean there were thirteen alphabets used. In this case, the first alphabet would begin with the letter "N", the second alphabet with the letter "E", and so on. The more alphabets, the more secure the cipher.

In the 18th century, when the monument was created, the most secure and well-known method of encrypting short messages or words was the polyalphabetic cipher. For longer communications, state-run black chambers often used nomenclature codes. Nomenclature codes were based on physical codebooks that had to be possessed by both parties and substituted whole words, syllables or phrases with coded counterparts. But for a small item such as a name, a polyalphabetic cipher was a more appropriate choice. First, it was very secure, as evidenced by its long-standing nickname, *"le chiffre indechiffrable."* Second, it lent itself to a shorter section of text and allowed sharing of the knowledge by communication of a simple key which would be used to decipher it. These keys were often made easy to remember by using a name (such as Nebucadnezzar) or a familiar poem or song to recall them. In fact, Beaufort's handwritten instructions for using the cipher specifically stated that the key should be a line of poetry or the name of a memorable person or place.[24]

Operating on the assumption that the most likely cipher used for the Shugborough inscription was a polyalphabetic substitution cipher (based on the functional requirements of a short, secure cipher and the historical availability of enciphering techniques at the time), we then approach the problem of the cipher's key. In theory, since a polyalphabetic cipher could use up to 8 different alphabets to encode the 8 letters, there are approximately 208 billion potential key combinations that could be used.

208 billion is a daunting number, and an 8-letter ciphertext is too short to crack using letter frequency analysis. However, we reduce these odds dramatically by using the historical information that is available. First, we know from the anonymous poem that the "mystic ciphers" conceal a name. Second, we know that it is a female name. Third, we know that it is an eight-letter name. Given that the number of eight-letter female names is finite, it is clear that we are now dealing with a more manageable amount of data.

We begin to define that data by establishing a list of goddess figures common in the western cultures of Greece, Rome, Egypt, Mesopotamia and Israel, as well as those common to the Celtic cultures of the British Isles. Pruning that down to those that are 8-letters long, we are left with 52 names. Then, to be more comprehensive in our analysis, we add all given female names common in England during the period of the monument's creation. Using historical UK parish marriage transcriptions from the years 1530 – 1830, we are able to produce a list of 434 additional female names, all of which are eight letters long (see appendix A for the complete lists of names). This leaves us with a combined total of 486 potential 8-letter names to evaluate.

As we have already discussed, a cipher such as this is basically a mathematical formula. Since we possess both the ciphertext and the 486 possible names in cleartext, we can reverse engineer the possible keys for each potential name. Knowing that there were two types of polyalphabetic cipher that were available at the time (the Vigenère and Sestri versions), and that each would produce a different key for the same name, we determine a total of 972 keys which would correspond to the 486 possible names. Although large, this is a much more manageable set of variables than the 208 billion we began with.

We then look at the 972 potential keys to determine whether any of them contain a recognizable pattern of repetition. Since short, repetitive patterns do not exist amongst the potential keys, we work under the assumption that the key is eight letters long. This is logical, since the longer the key the greater the security, and eight would be the longest number of characters that could be used on a cipher that is eight characters long.

Now our task becomes the examination of the potential keys to look for the types of patterns recommended by Beaufort for use as a key. These could be a name, a combination of words or an acrostic taken from a poem or song. We begin this task by looking at the keys associated with the names of western goddess figures, since we know the Shepherdess is somehow working within the tradition of western syncretism. Here is an example of how this looks:

Name								Key 1 Vigenère								Key 2 Sestri							
1	2	3	4	5	6	7	8	1	2	3	4	5	6	7	8	1	2	3	4	5	6	7	8
C	a	l	l	i	o	p	e	M	U	D	H	N	M	G	R	L	T	C	G	M	L	F	Q
D	e	s	p	o	i	n	a	L	Q	W	D	H	S	I	V	K	P	V	C	G	R	H	U
R	h	i	a	n	n	o	n	X	N	G	S	I	N	H	I	W	M	F	R	H	M	G	H
S	h	e	k	i	n	a	h	W	N	K	I	N	N	V	O	V	M	J	H	M	M	U	N

Table 1: Eight-letter female names and their corresponding keys (using Vigenère and Sestri ciphers).

Upon close inspection of the 104 keys that we have produced through our reverse engineering of the 52 goddess figures' names, the initial result reveals that there is not a single name which produces an easy to recognize one-word key. We then continue to produce keys for the comprehensive list of names, generating a grand-total of 972 keys to examine. Again, we find that none of the results consist of a one-word key.

The next step in our analysis of the keys is to look for patterns that may indicate the use of multiple words or an acrostic taken from a poem or song. We find the types of fragments and short words that any random sampling of text may generate. Seeking to refine our search for a more focused analysis, we take all keys with a four-letter word or longer and examine them more closely. The process does produce a few results, some of which warrant more attention. The following table provides a short list of the keys which contained interesting components such as easily recognizable words:

Name								Key							
1	2	3	4	5	6	7	8	1	2	3	4	5	6	7	8
A	n	g	e	r	o	n	a	O	H	I	O	E	M	I	V
A	t	a	e	g	i	n	a	O	B	O	O	P	S	I	V
D	e	b	r	a	n	u	a	K	P	M	A	U	M	A	U
N	e	v	e	r	i	t	a	B	Q	T	O	E	S	C	V
B	e	t	t	r	i	c	e	N	Q	V	Z	E	S	T	R
B	r	i	d	g	g	e	t	M	C	F	O	O	T	Q	B
M	a	g	d	a	l	e	n	B	T	H	O	U	O	Q	H
M	a	g	d	a	l	l	e	B	T	H	O	U	O	J	Q
A	r	a	b	a	e	l	l	O	D	O	R	V	W	K	K
C	h	a	t	h	e	r	i	M	N	O	Z	O	W	E	N
C	i	s	s	e	l	e	y	M	M	W	A	R	P	R	X
F	a	r	b	r	i	c	k	J	U	X	R	E	S	T	L
M	i	l	d	r	e	d	a	C	M	D	P	E	W	S	V
R	u	d	e	r	f	o	r	X	A	L	O	E	V	H	E
S	i	s	s	e	l	i	e	W	M	W	A	R	P	N	R
S	y	s	s	e	l	l	y	W	W	W	A	R	P	K	X

Table 2: Keys containing unique recognizable patterns.

In evaluating these patterns, some are more compelling than others. The last eight names do not have a strong spiritual connotation, and neither do the words in their keys. The first eight names, however, are those of goddess figures or women associated with the Judeo-Christian religious tradition. Nevertheless, the words in most of them are hardly compelling, and feel more like we are grasping at straws.

However, upon close inspection, one of the keys which contains the word THOU is very noteworthy. The Letters BTHOUOQH contain the triad OQH. In examining the tradition of divine or semi-divine feminine figures, we know that the title Queen of Heaven is almost universally applied, from Isis to biblical references to Astarte and on to the Blessed Virgin Mary. Now we have an interesting pattern with a thematic tie to our subject.

But the solution becomes clearer when we realize that the clue has been before us all along, in the anonymous description of the Shepherdess's Tomb left to us by one of Thomas Anson's circle. At the very moment that the author refers to the "mystic ciphers" that conceal the Shepherdess's name, the author formally alludes to Apuleius' *Metamorphosis*. And not just any part of *The Metamorphosis*, but the exact moment when the protagonist pleadingly addresses Isis by name. And in addressing her, he begins, "O Queen of Heaven, be thou…", continuing on with a long list of her syncretic names from various classical cultures. The poetic muse has, in fact, hidden a hint at the key without actually writing it down. BTHOUOQH appears to stand for some form of the phrase "Blessed be Thou, O Queen of Heaven." Would Thomas Anson have understood? Certainly. Would strangers be unfamiliar with the cipher? Not unless they had generated every possible key and painstakingly examined them, and then only if they understood the bigger ideas at play in the monument itself.

The key stands out because both the key and the name it produces contain similar thematic elements, and likewise connect to the greater esoteric concepts at work in the monument. Of the 978 potential keys, only one works uniformly within the western mystery tradition, its reverence for divine names, and the concept of syncretic female types with the historical significance of a tomb in the garden. MAGDALEN is the name with which Thomas Anson addresses his Shepherdess. But we have more work to do to examine this idea.

THE ACROSTIC
INVOCATION FORMULA

As we have explained, the key to the encryption is an acrostic cipher, most likely taken from a phrase like "Blessed be THOU, O Queen of Heaven." It is an interesting conclusion, but before we examine it we must finish the exploration of the acrostic key.

At first glance, this particular acrostic may seem odd and perhaps contrived. Why would the inventor of this cipher use some individual letters to form the key, but also include an entire four-letter word? Many acrostics use a more regular pattern, such as the lead letters in each stanza, capitalized letters or the lead letters in each word. The selection of the individual lead capital letters makes sense, and there is a possibility that one would capitalize all letters of the pronoun "thou" if it was referring to a divine being. Nevertheless, one must question the level of certainty given by a solution whose key is potentially divided into two patterns: a four-letter word and four individual letters.

Fortunately, there is an explanation for this unique pattern, found in the western esoteric tradition that influenced the design of the monument. Renaissance scholars often sought to identify parallels between the mystical elements of different esoteric traditions. Many, like Pico della Mirandola and Johannes Reuchlin, lauded the spiritual power of hidden divine names. These names were extracted as acrostics from the Davidic Psalms using Kabbalistic techniques. This practice became a core element of the Christian Kabbalist tradition, further explored and written about by men such as Cornelius Agrippa and the renowned Jesuit, Athanasius Kircher.

In Kircher's *Oedipus Aegyptachus*, he discussed the accepted invocation formulas for deriving 72 names of God from the Davidic Psalms.[25] These formulas allowed one to extract a divine name from its hiding place within a Davidic Psalm, and in so doing engaged the divine name in a mystical operation. In every example, the Divine name was constructed out of two patterns: the four letter Tetragrammaton YHWH, and three additional letters taken from words in the remainder of the Psalm. This is the pattern which the acrostic key for the Shugborough monument used. One four-letter word, the pronoun "THOU", directly addresses the lauded figure, and a balance of individual letters account for the rest of the invocation formula. Thus, the unique acrostic used to generate the key is quite congruent when understood in the context of and in revealing a divine name from the Hebrew Psalms via Kabbalistic means.

Once we possess the appropriate key, we can move to the conclusion of the decrypting process. The key is applied to the ciphertext according to the rules of the Sestri polyalphabetic cipher. The first letter of the key is located in the left hand side of the grid. Moving across to the right within that row, the column that contains the first letter of the ciphertext is found. The cryptologist then follows that column of the square up to the top and selects the letter that appears in the uppermost row of the column. This step is followed with each successive letter of the key and script. Once the ciphertext is completely decoded, using the Sestri square and the aforementioned key, the remaining cleartext reveals the name of the Shepherdess: MAGDALEN.

Shugborough Cipher Tableau

Z	Y	X	W	V	U	T	S	R	Q	P	O	N	M	L	K	J	I	H	G	F	E	D	C	B	A
A	Z	Y	X	W	V	U	T	S	R	Q	P	O	N	M	L	K	J	I	H	G	F	E	D	C	B
B	A	Z	Y	X	W	V	U	T	S	R	Q	P	O	N	M	L	K	J	I	H	G	F	E	D	C
C	B	A	Z	Y	X	W	V	U	T	S	R	Q	P	O	N	M	L	K	J	I	H	G	F	E	D
D	C	B	A	Z	Y	X	W	V	U	T	S	R	Q	P	O	N	M	L	K	J	I	H	G	F	E
E	D	C	B	A	Z	Y	X	W	V	U	T	S	R	Q	P	O	N	M	L	K	J	I	H	G	F
F	E	D	C	B	A	Z	Y	X	W	V	U	T	S	R	Q	P	O	N	M	L	K	J	I	H	G
G	F	E	D	C	B	A	Z	Y	X	W	V	U	T	S	R	Q	P	O	N	M	L	K	J	I	H
H	G	F	E	D	C	B	A	Z	Y	X	W	V	U	T	S	R	Q	P	O	N	M	L	K	J	I
I	H	G	F	E	D	C	B	A	Z	Y	X	W	V	U	T	S	R	Q	P	O	N	M	L	K	J
J	I	H	G	F	E	D	C	B	A	Z	Y	X	W	V	U	T	S	R	Q	P	O	N	M	L	K
K	J	I	H	G	F	E	D	C	B	A	Z	Y	X	W	V	U	T	S	R	Q	P	O	N	M	L
L	K	J	I	H	G	F	E	D	C	B	A	Z	Y	X	W	V	U	T	S	R	Q	P	O	N	M
M	L	K	J	I	H	G	F	E	D	C	B	A	Z	Y	X	W	V	U	T	S	R	Q	P	O	N
N	M	L	K	J	I	H	G	F	E	D	C	B	A	Z	Y	X	W	V	U	T	S	R	Q	P	O
O	N	M	L	K	J	I	H	G	F	E	D	C	B	A	Z	Y	X	W	V	U	T	S	R	Q	P
P	O	N	M	L	K	J	I	H	G	F	E	D	C	B	A	Z	Y	X	W	V	U	T	S	R	Q
Q	P	O	N	M	L	K	J	I	H	G	F	E	D	C	B	A	Z	Y	X	W	V	U	T	S	R
R	Q	P	O	N	M	L	K	J	I	H	G	F	E	D	C	B	A	Z	Y	X	W	V	U	T	S
S	R	Q	P	O	N	M	L	K	J	I	H	G	F	E	D	C	B	A	Z	Y	X	W	V	U	T
T	S	R	Q	P	O	N	M	L	K	J	I	H	G	F	E	D	C	B	A	Z	Y	X	W	V	U
U	T	S	R	Q	P	O	N	M	L	K	J	I	H	G	F	E	D	C	B	A	Z	Y	X	W	V
V	U	T	S	R	Q	P	O	N	M	L	K	J	I	H	G	F	E	D	C	B	A	Z	Y	X	W
W	V	U	T	S	R	Q	P	O	N	M	L	K	J	I	H	G	F	E	D	C	B	A	Z	Y	X
X	W	V	U	T	S	R	Q	P	O	N	M	L	K	J	I	H	G	F	E	D	C	B	A	Z	Y
Y	X	W	V	U	T	S	R	Q	P	O	N	M	L	K	J	I	H	G	F	E	D	C	B	A	Z

MAGDALEN

KEY	CIPHERTEXT	PLAINTEXT
B	O	M
T	U	A
H	O	G
O	S	D
U	V	A
O	A	L
Q	V	E
H	V	N

Table 3: The Sestri cipher tableau (left) and the ciphertext, key and plaintext solution (right).

The Shepherd's Monument, then, is a funerary altar sacred to the figure of Mary Magdalen. Moreover, the monument represents her symbolically as a shepherdess, operating in the syncretic tradition of Isis, Diana and other sacred female spiritual types. It uses an acrostic key taken from another sacred female figure: the Virgin Mary. It uses an invocation formula from the Christian Kabbalistic tradition to extract the key. And just as Mary Magdalen is best remembered for her discovery at the garden tomb on Easter morning, so is she here memorialized at the mysterious tomb in Thomas Anson's gardens. And building on this theme, she is memorialized contemplating a tomb that itself incorporates funerary elements of different cultures: the pyramid, sarcophagus and sepulcher, stressing the syncretic interpretation of her role.

The text of the anonymous Shugborough poem of 1767 supports the theory by identifying the Shepherdess as the object of the shrine and by indicating that her name has been hidden in it with ciphers. And, more importantly, by hinting at the cipher's key itself in the allusion to Apuleius. And now, we are finally able to discern that the ciphers, when unlocked, reveal the Shepherdess to be Mary Magdalen.

THE KEY AND ITS POSSIBLE SOURCES

We do not know the source of the key, and we may never know it. Perhaps access to the private Anson family library might give us a clue. There are several possibilities we know of. Certainly it could be a unique phrase developed for the monument by Thomas Anson. It could also be derivative of many historical forms of Marian devotion. The medieval English hymn "Edi be thu" or "Blessed be Thou, O Queen of Heaven" is a valid possibility. Another possible source of the key is a Lady Psalter sometimes attributed to Saint Bonaventure, which was often used by Protestant theologians to support accusations of goddess worship within the Catholic Church. The *Psalter of the Blessed Virgin Mary* is a feminine, Christian mirror of the traditional Davidic book of Psalms. It accomplishes this reflection in form and content, by consisting of exactly 150 Psalms, like the biblical book, but these Psalms are dedicated to the female figure of the Virgin Mary, instead of the traditional male God YHWH.

This psalter is less well-known today, but in Anson's time it was often referenced in the theological disputes between Catholics and Protestants. Many Protestant writers passionately pointed to the psalter as evidence of Catholic goddess worship. Bishop Stillingfleet, grandfather of Thomas Anson's close friend Benjamin Stillingfleet, was one of those who vehemently denounced the practice of Marian devotion, and who specifically referenced Bonaventure's psalter in his own writings.[26] As did John Foxe, whose *Foxe's Acts and Monuments* was at one point a required text in all English churches. Anson would have undoubtedly been aware of the work, and with his interest in both syncretism and the Isis figure, the psalter may have presented a path to find the sacred feminine concept alive in Christianity.

The letters that make up the key would be taken from Psalm 43 of the *Psalter of the Blessed Virgin Mary*, which reads:

O Lady, we have heard with our ears: and our fathers
have told it unto us.
For thy merits are ineffable: and thy wonders
exceedingly stupendous.
O Lady, innumerable are thy virtues: and inestimable
are thy mercies.
Exult, O my soul, and rejoice in her: for many good
things
are prepared for those who praise her.
Blessed be thou, O Queen of the Heavens and the
angels: and let those who praise thy magnificence be
blessed by God.[27]

If this is the source, it would fit neatly into renaissance magus Cornelius Agrippa's description of the types of hymns used in mystic rites:[28] the first four stanzas are laudatory and descriptive of the characteristics of Mary, but the fifth stanza stands out, as it culminates the verse by actively invoking a blessing upon her. Furthermore, it then petitions for a return of the blessing upon those who honor her. It extols the qualities of the figure, blesses the figure, and asks for a return of the blessing. Moreover, the key to unlocking the sacred name on the monument resides in the Psalm, just as the Kabbalistic names of God are encoded in the acrostics of the traditional Davidic Psalms.

But why? Why the monument and why the complex, esoteric system of encrypting the name? And what exactly is the mystic tie-in of it all?

We cannot provide indisputable answers to these questions. There is just not enough historical evidence. We see patterns, like shadows on a wall, but nothing as clear as we would hope for. And the answers that we do surmise, the theories that we may propose, will undoubtedly contain some elements which are somewhat accurate and some which are absolutely incorrect. Nevertheless, having come this far, it is worth some educated conjecture at this time to try and reach a better understanding of the monument and its mystery.

---

[5] Anonymous Poem of 1767, Records of the Anson Family of Shugborough, Earls of Lichfield, Staffordshire Hall of Records.

[6] *A Catalogue of the Splendid Property at Shugborough Hall, Stafford to be Sold at Auction...on the Premises on Monday the 1st Day of August 1842.* William Salt Library. Ref: SC B/1/1.

[7] Jean Baptiste Du Bos, *Critical Reflections on Poetry, Painting and Music,* trans. Thomas Nugent (London: John Nourse, 1748), 45.

[8] Ovid, *Tristia,* 3.13.21-22.

[9] Vergil, *Aeneid,* 3:63-64.

[10] Sir William Bagot, Unpublished Poem. Staffordshire Record Office. Anson Papers. Ref: D615/P (S)/2/5.

[11] Percy Gardner, *Sculptured Tombs of Hellas.* (New York: The MacMillan Company, 1896), 2.

[12] J. M. C. Toynbee, *Death and Burial in the Roman World*, (Cornell University Press. 1971), 246-247.

[13] Toynbee, 35.

[14] Anonymous Poem of 1767, Records of the Anson Family of Shugborough, Earls of Lichfield, Staffordshire Hall of Records.

[15] *A Catalogue of the Splendid Property at Shugborough Hall, Stafford to be Sold at Auction...on the Premises on Monday the 1st Day of August 1842.* William Salt Library. Rcf: SC B/1/1.

[16] Apuleius, *The Golden Ass: or, a Book of Changes*, trans. Joel C. Relihan (Indiana: Hackett Publishing, 2007), 233-234.

[17] Anonymous Poem of 1767, Records of the Anson Family of Shugborough, Earls of Lichfield, Staffordshire Hall of Records.

[18] *A Catalogue of the Splendid Property at Shugborough Hall, Stafford to be Sold at Auction...on the Premises on Monday the 1st Day of August 1842.* William Salt Library. Ref: SC B/1/1.

[19] Pausanias, *Description of Greece* 8. 37. 1 - 8. 38. 2.

[20] Giacomo Chevalier De Seingalt Casanova, *The Complete Memoirs of Casanova the Story of My Life.* (Oxford: Benediction Classics, 2013), 415.

[21] Casanova, 417.

[22] Casanova, 417.

[23] Brian J. Winkel, "Casanova and the Beaufort Cipher," *Cryptologia* 2:2 (1978): 161-163.

[24] Kahn, 202.

[25] Athanasius Kircher, *Oedipus Aegyptiacus* (1652), section Classis IV - Cabala Hebraeorum, 275-280.

[26] Benjamin Stillingfleet, *A Discourse Concerning the Idolatry Practised in the Church of Rome*, 2nd Ed,. (London: Robert White, 1672), 163.

[27] Saint Bonaventure. *The Psalter of the Blessed Virgin Mary.* Ps. XLIII.

[28] Cornelius Agrippa, *Three Books of Occult Philosophy*, Book I (Printed by R.W. for Gregory Moule: London, 1651), Chapters LXX and LXXI.

PART TWO

Understanding The Shepherd's Monument

Understanding The Shepherd's Monument

One can solve a cipher and still be left with many questions. The cleartext is much like a math problem: knowing that an answer is 42 tells us very little about the path one followed to get there, and the context within which the problem operated to reach such a conclusion. What does the 42 signify? 42 apples? 42 seconds before the end of the world? A numerical definition of the meaning of life?

Just as context lends greater understanding to something as simple as a math problem, we need to establish context to better understand what the name MAGDALEN meant to Thomas Anson, and to begin to fathom just why he built a beautiful, mysterious monument to both revere and conceal it. As with any work of art, symbol or sign, the Shepherdess's Tomb is communicating an idea. And any idea powerful enough to be both revered and concealed cannot exist in a vacuum. It must, therefore, also take up residence in other aspects of the owner's life, and be expressed in other ways.

In order to understand the ideas at work in Thomas Anson's life, we need to step back into mid eighteenth-century England and get a sense for both Thomas Anson and his peers. We need to understand their special interests, as well as the philosophies and beliefs being explored at the time. From gentlemen's clubs to secret societies, mystery schools to mysticism, orientalism and syncretism, there was a lot going on and Thomas Anson was involved and interested in a great deal of it. To begin, we will travel back to London on the eve of the Winter Solstice in 1742.

THE EGYPTIAN SOCIETY'S
FESTIVAL OF ISIS

Figure 9: Saint James Square, London, c. 1752

On Dec. 11, 1742, the air in St. James square was chilly and full of the sounds and smells of the Christmas season. Carriages escorted Lords and Ladies to formal functions full of holiday fare. As guests arrived at the townhouses faint echoes of Handel escaped the open doors, originating from unseen drawing rooms within. However, in another part of London there was a very different celebration taking place. At this exclusive gathering, a group of wealthy English gentlemen and scholars had come together for a more exotic affair. And in this affair we find evidence of two concepts which are both vital to a better understanding of the Shepherd's Monument: mystery schools and syncretism.

As the December sun was setting against the London skyline, the thirty or so members arrived at their private banquet decked out in Eastern attire. Some dressed in turbans and black camissas; adorned with gold on their ankles, necks, ears, or noses. They addressed one another with varying titles of Arabic, Persian and Turkish origin. The secretary was the *Reis Effendi* and the president held the title of *Sheik*, others were the *Hasnedar, Mohausil,* and *Gumrocjee.* The air was filled with the odor of incense and was now and again pierced by the jangling noise of the Sheik's Egyptian sistrum, a ceremonial instrument that served as his staff of office.[29]

The sistrum always accompanied the goddess Isis in Egyptian artwork, and it was no accident that the Sheik bore the same instrument in his hand, for tonight was also the evening of the Winter Solstice,[30] the traditional celebration of the Feast of Isis. This organization was none other than the Egyptian Society, an exclusive organization founded in 1741 and made up of early Romantics who held the study of Egyptian culture as a potential source of profound wisdom.[31] Moreover, this was a serious organization whose members had traveled to Egypt and the Middle East during a time when such a trip was not a learning holiday, but an oftentimes perilous undertaking.[32]

Here were men like the anthropologist Dr. Richard Pococke, antiquarian Martin Folkes, the well-travelled romantic Lord Sandwich, and Dr. William Stukeley, who pioneered the field of archaeology with his groundbreaking examination of Stonehenge. And though the club held meetings regularly every fortnight, this was the one gathering when every member was bound by their laws to attend: to celebrate the Feast of Isis on the same day it had been celebrated for thousands of years, a day which also marked the anniversary of the club's founding.[33] On this particular evening, Dr. Stukeley delivered a lecture proposing a syncretic connection between the origin of the Feast of Isis in Egypt and other world religions, ultimately striving to connect the date to the religious traditions of England's ancient Druids.[34]

Figure 10: Description of the Egyptian goddess Isis, including the names which other cultures have applied to her syncretic figure. From Athanasius Kircher's *Oedipus Aegyptachus*.

The celebration of the Egyptian Society was a small example of the type of activity that wealthy English nobles engaged in during this period of enlightenment and affluence. The general interest in clubs and social organizations was, in many cases, a matter of "keeping up with the Joneses" throughout the social circuit. However, whether consciously recognized or not, the activities of groups such as the Egyptian Society allowed members to engage their philosophical interests in actual participatory experience. For some, especially those whose philosophy challenged the individual to act upon their will, this was also a part of the lure. The marriage of a modern discourse on ideas with active participation in ancient ritual was borne largely out of the concept of ancient western mystery schools. A common feature in the world of western esotericism, it is necessary to understand the mystery school to more fully comprehend the social, yet mysterious and exclusive nature of the Shepherd's Monument.

MYSTERY SCHOOLS

Mystery schools form the organizational basis of most western esoteric religious practices. They are framed around the idea that most religions have an exoteric, or outer level of belief, which revolves around outward symbols and rituals. The exoteric beliefs are widely accepted and followed by the masses of believers. However, an inner, esoteric level of belief also exists and is reserved for the few who are initiated into the "mysteries" of the religion. Those initiated into the mysteries receive knowledge that is hidden from the masses. According to their beliefs, this often includes a deeper level of understanding of the true meaning of exoteric symbols and practices, as well as rituals only known to the inner circle. There is typically no written body of knowledge, and the school is not a competing religion but rather a cult associated with existing mainstream religions of the culture it belongs to.

The most widely known western mystery schools are the pagan traditions of ancient Greece and Egypt. Some of the chief Greek mystery schools are the Eleusinian, Orphic and Dionysian mysteries. Others that stand out in the pagan world were the Egyptian mysteries of Isis and the Mithraic mysteries of Rome. However, within the Judeo-Christian tradition there are also elements of the mystery tradition.

For example, the Hebrew tradition of Kabbalah is in many ways a mystery school. The Kabbalistic tradition has a strong component of concealed knowledge, such as sacred names hidden within the text of the Hebrew scripture. Many Gnostic Christian sects of the first few centuries AD also contained elements that were common to pagan mystery schools, such as the revelation of concealed knowledge to the inner circle, as well as the ability to connect the human with the divine while still living in the material world. Moreover, there are some basic esoteric elements that are discernible even in the teaching methods of the New Testament, such as the communication of parables to large groups of people and the explanation of them in private amongst the disciples.

This concept of inner, esoteric traditions is vital to understanding the social context of the Shepherd's Monument. At the time of the monument's creation, organizations founded on the basic concepts of the mystery school were flourishing in Europe. Perhaps the best example is that of speculative freemasonry, which was proliferating throughout England, France, through central Europe and into Russia. Many of Thomas Anson's associates were leaders within the Masonic movement, including Martin Folkes, John Byrom and William Stukeley. Others close to Anson, such as Lord Sandwich and Francis

Dashwood, founded smaller, more exclusive organizations modeled after the pagan mystery schools.

For example, Francis Dashwood's infamous Monks of Medmenham, better known as the Hellfire Club, became the subject of bawdy speculation and scandal for years. Dashwood, like Anson, had used his wealth and artistic connections to customize the architecture and artwork on his property to suit his private interests. His projects included the conversion of the Medmenham Abbey into a Pagan Temple to revel and celebrate the *Bona Dea*, or Great Mother Goddess. He also had a series of caves excavated into a secretive underground banquet hall where both licentious and

Figure 11: William Hogarth's 1750's portrait of Francis Dashwood as a parody of Saint Francis of Assisi. Dashwood is meditating over an erotic novel, while Lord Sandwich peers over his shoulder from within the halo.

pagan ceremonies were rumored to have taken place. Though members were sworn to secrecy in the tradition of Harpocrates, onetime member John Wilkes likened the candid goings-on to the private celebration of "English Eleusinian Mysteries."[35] And indeed, the plethora of clubs and fraternal organizations popularized in eighteenth century England often drew on the tradition of mystery schools for the genesis of their rites, initiations and exclusive nature.

Did Thomas Anson participate? We have no record of whether or not he was a freemason or a member of Dashwood's Monks, but he did participate in a number of exclusive organizations rich in the spirit of mystery, ritual and fraternity, and in so doing he became more closely associated with people like Dashwood, Sandwich, Folkes, and Stukeley.

In addition to the Egyptian Society, Thomas Anson also belonged to the Divan Club, whose members enjoyed exclusive meetings focused on the study of Eastern culture. Anson was nominated into the club by Lord Sandwich, his neighbor. Later, Anson joined Sandwich and Dashwood at the Society of Dilettanti, which revered the cultures of ancient Greece and Rome. Finally, Anson was also a member of the Royal Society, a scientific organization with historical roots in the Rosicrucian tradition of the 17th century, and which was dominated by freemasons during its first century of development.

The reason this all contributes towards a better understanding of the Shepherd's Monument is that the monument openly declares, by its unique symbolism and inscription, that there is a secret before us. Furthermore, the open display of the coded inscription makes no attempt to hide this fact. There is a mystery being transmitted before us, but we are not in the exclusive club that understands its nature. It is unlikely that the monument was understood only by Thomas Anson, as several of his peers have hinted at a special level of meaning hidden behind the ciphers. Nevertheless, which subset of his associates might have shared the knowledge, having been "initiated" into its mysteries, is pure conjecture.

THE KIRCHER INFLUENCE

The mysteries of the Egyptian Society are yet another example of the connections between Thomas Anson and the seventeenth century scholar Athanasius Kircher. We have already seen how the ideas expressed in Kircher's *Oedipus Aegyptachus* come into play in several parts of the mystery's solution. Although we have no way to directly substantiate the claim that Anson borrowed these ideas from Kircher, it is clear that Kircher's work was hugely important to all serious Egyptian scholars of the time.

Figure 12: Athanasius Kircher, from the frontispiece of Giorgio de Sepibus's 1678 work, *Romani Collegii Societatis Jesu Musaeum Celeberrimum.*

Anson's membership in the Egyptian Society, his expression of Egyptian culture in the artwork on his estate and Anson's own personal travels to Egypt and the Levant demonstrate a strong passion, which very likely led him to be intimately familiar with Kircher and his ideas. We know Anson maintained Kircher's work in his own library at Shugborough, and it seems clear that at some point in Anson's early years, he became richly enamored with the culture of Egypt and the near east.

With a tutor like William Jones Sr., one cannot blame Anson for this spark of interest. There are signs that Jones may have accompanied Anson on at least one of his voyages to the Levant. Moreover, we have evidence that Jones was especially interested in Kircher's work and its syncretic ideas. Below is an image of extensive notes found in the inner jacket of a book on Kabbalah, recently sold in an auction of the Macclesfield Library. This book was owned by Thomas Anson's uncle and was probably given to him by William Jones Sr., Anson's tutor, who also proposed Anson for membership in the Royal Society. The handwritten notes are in English, Greek, Hebrew and Latin, and they indicate in-depth knowledge of both the Kabbalah and hermetic teachings expressed by Iamblichus, Athanasius Kircher and Johannes Reuchlin.

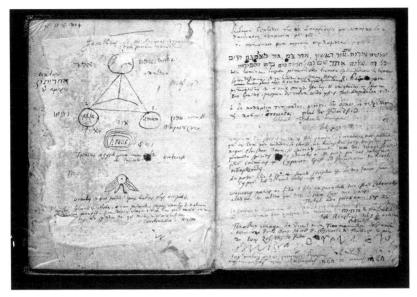

Figure 13: Handwritten notes detailing Kircher's syncretic equating of the Christian trinity with Egyptian gods. Kabbalist work *Sephir Yetzirah* in the Library of the Earls of Macclesfield. Courtesy of the Sotheby's Picture Library.

The hand-drawn triangular symbol on the left page is copied from a diagram found in *Oedipus Egyptachus*. It represents a syncretic equating of the Christian trinity of Father, Son and Holy Spirit with Egyptian divinities. Kircher's work is a powerful example of the type of syncretic thought which was prevalent in Anson's time, and which sought to find connections between pagan, Jewish and Christian traditions. By connecting the mystical elements of Egyptian, Jewish and Christian religion under a hermetic philosophy, Kircher sought, like other Christian Kabbalists before him, to find splinters of truth in all world religions that were ultimately realized more completely in the Christian faith.

In doing so, Kircher worked within and referenced the long-standing tradition of syncretism that had been developed in antiquity. And in establishing a scholarly examination of these ideas, he laid a foundation that would later be built upon by others like Sir James Frazer, whose publication of *The Golden Bough* in 1890 was a key milestone in the development of the modern study of Comparative Religion.

So where else do the connections between Thomas Anson and Kircher lie? For one, we know that the invocation formula used to unlock the name on the monument appears to be based on that which is detailed in *Oedipus Aegyptachus*. The basic architecture of Anson's cipher key is taken from the Kabbalistic keys, which Kircher describes as extracting the 72 divine names of God from the book of Psalms. Moreover, in this work Kircher also explores the use of polyalphabetic ciphers, referencing the construction of them by the venerated abbot Johannes Trithemius of Sponheim. The nature of the Shepherdess mystery appears strongly rooted in the hermetic Christian Kabbalistic tradition, and Kircher provides detailed insights into many aspects of this knowledge.

But there is more knowledge that Kircher transmits in this work. In his exploration of syncretism, Kircher examines in detail the ideas of Iamblichus, who sought to combine and revitalize the pagan traditions of the western world into a more unified tradition. Iamblichus sought to do this with a return to the active practice of theurgy, a ritual form of worship that enables the practitioner to achieve divine gnosis. But Kircher takes the ideas a step forward from Iamblichus, looking at the similarities between pagan traditions and Judeo-Christian theology, seeking to display the common elements of all.

And there is no more syncretic figure than Shugborough's Shepherdess as described to us in the poem: known by many names in many lands. With this vantage point, the addition of the Jewish Ossuary and the Egyptian Pyramid to the Greek

Sarcophagus on the Poussin relief makes perfect sense. The Shepherdess is a syncretic version of the divine feminine goddess figure, mourning at the tomb of the dying male god, whatever his country. And in the Christian tradition there is no more fitting woman than Mary Magdalen, whose most powerful defining moment takes place in the garden on Easter morning, at the tomb of the rising God.

Figure 14: Close up of the marble frieze, displaying the curious ossuary and pyramid that have been added to the original sarcophagus. Courtesy of Andrew Baker.

THEURGY

If we are to accept the idea that the Shepherd's Monument is associated with a goddess figure whose name is cleverly kept secret; and if we are furthermore to accept the idea that knowledge of the name constitutes some type of initiation into an exclusive community of belief; we are still led back to the inescapable question: what is the monument for?

The answer may lie in the ancient religious practice of theurgy. Theurgy is taken from the Greek *theourgia*, which means "work of the gods." It is no less than the unification of man with the divine, through ceremonial mystic ritual, ultimately achieving a temporary perfection of the soul. In Christian religion, one of the best-known examples of theurgy is found in Dante's relation of the beatific vision. He experiences it at the climax of his *Divine Comedy*, when he sings hymns to the Virgin Mary and is finally enabled to ascend to the point that he achieves mystic union with God.

In pagan mystery schools as well as some Gnostic Christian sects, theurgy represented the highest level of spiritual growth and was often deemed necessary in order to attain salvation in the afterlife. The experiences related in both Apuleius and Dante's works are from dramatically different traditions. However, both constitute examples of theurgic ascent; and in both practices it is a feminine being of divine or semi-divine status, a Queen of Heaven, that enables the protagonist to achieve it. In Apuleius' tale it is the goddess Isis. In Dante's it is the Virgin Mary. For another example we may look at the *Chaldean Oracles*, in which the goddess Hekate is invoked as a gatekeeper who is vital to the soul's journey from the material realm up into the heavens. In each example there is a being in a higher level of the celestial hierarchy who must be invoked in order to accomplish the operation.

Figure 15: Gustave Doré's 19th century portrayal of Dante's beatific vision.

Though the intermediary invoked in theurgic operations need not be feminine, I have chosen these examples as they were all known by Anson. In each case the goddess figure plays a key role as a guide or conduit who helps the human temporarily escape the bonds of the material world in a quest to reach the zenith of the spiritual world; attaining knowledge of the ineffable, or gnosis. Each example, however, relies on a spiritual worldview rooted in Platonic philosophy, and that is worth a short comment.

In a Platonic or Neoplatonic worldview, God is seen as the creator of all things, but as a creator who accomplished the task through a series of emanations. In each emanation, beings were created (such as lesser gods, angels, aieons or daimones, depending on the culture) who were given demiurgic power over the emanation below them, until the lowest emanation of these successive spheres created the material world. Thus, the material world was the farthest away from the purest nature of God, but through using mystic rituals to establish sympathetic connections with beings in the spheres above the earth, mankind could aspire to spiritually unite back with the great creator.

This type of Platonic worldview was vital to the ancient cultures of Greece, Rome and Egypt. What's more, it was the worldview that was understood, lived and felt by Christians for many, many years. One can see parallels in the ways angels and saints took on roles of mediators in the Catholic Church, becoming semi-divine beings who provided the same type of sympathetic connection between mankind and the Father. With the rebirth of Neoplatonic ideas during the Renaissance, the influence of this concept became even greater.

Theurgy relied on a Platonic or Neoplatonic worldview, but as Enlightenment concepts such as humanism and the scientific revolution began to grow, the acceptance and influence of Neoplatonic thought began to decline. Intellectual circles had once championed such thinking, because in many ways the resurgence of Neoplatonic ideas had dared to question the existing intellectual status quo. Now, however, the advent of the scientific method and the results that it produced had made the Neoplatonic worldview irrelevant in the eyes of the scientific elite. A noble notion of idealism, at best; the concept of man's ability to bridge the gap between the real and the ideal became anathema to the learned scientific community. That type of idealism was now relegated to the arts, where it eventually found new life in the birth of Romanticism, and to the underground world of 19th century esoteric mysticism and the occult.

Thus, during Anson's life, serious acceptance of Neoplatonic philosophy was in a state of general decline. Nevertheless, it was not dead. Moreover, those who championed it could be quite passionate. Though labeled as rakes, the members of the Hellfire Club were at the highest levels of society and they held strong Neoplatonic beliefs. Neoplatonic ideas also had a home in the communities of mystics who gathered in London and other niche areas of Europe. Denmark had a strong Jewish community whose Kabbalistic ideas also emigrated to London with the teaching of Jacob Frank. Religious sects such as the Philadelphian Society and the Swedenborgians had Gnostic components as key parts of their beliefs. In Lyons, Martinez de Pasqually originated the school of Martinism, which practiced theurgy as a central component of its belief in the reintegration of mankind. Moreover, those who led the way in the Greek revival, like Anson, also appear to have had sympathies with not only a general Neoplatonic perspective but theurgic practice, as well. It is interesting to note that Thomas Taylor, the great translator who moved in Anson's circles, made a point of translating the *Chaldean Oracles* and Iamblichus' *On the Mysteries of the Egyptians*, arguably two of the most valuable texts in the study of classical theurgy.

Earlier in this essay we established that the artistic design of the Shepherd's Monument appears to be a funerary altar set in the form of a Greco-Roman stele, conceived by someone whose personal philosophy was strongly rooted in Neoplatonic ideas. As such, the monument was capable of serving as a type of *sunthemata*. *Sunthemata* is a Greek term, used to describe a symbol which aided in the practice of ritual theurgy. The lowest level of *sunthemata* are physical objects, such as the stone monument itself. These physical forms begin to establish a sympathetic connection between the individual and the divine entity being engaged. The next levels are divine names, such as that encrypted on the tomb. From there the next level was mathematical, such as the formula used to decipher the name, or the geometric principles used in the design of the artwork. Whether the theurgic practice was conducted in group ritual or as a solitary form of contemplation, (a question we may never have an answer to) the same spiritual goal of elevation towards mystic union with the divine was assisted through multiple aspects of this unique work of art.

Just as both syncretism and the concept of mystery schools are vital to the thematic structure of the monument, theurgy may lie at the heart of its practical design. The Shepherdess is indeed a representation of the feminine divine principle, and as such represents a mediator who, engaged properly, has the potential to help one attain mystic gnosis. This is the purpose that the monument served, and understanding this concept helps illuminate the motivation behind its curious features.

When Iamblichus revitalized theurgy throughout the pagan world, it took place during a period when Christianity was on the rise and the traditional polytheism of the Mediterranean world was in decline. Nevertheless, Iamblichus does not present himself as an enemy of Christianity, but rather as one who would challenge the current state of affairs in pagan worship.

In Iamblichus' eyes, the issue in the pagan world was that contemplative philosophy had replaced active participatory worship. The Platonic schools of the time had distanced the physical world from a key role in spiritual ascent, and as a result religious practice had lost its vitality. Iamblichus sought to unite the similar aspects of different pagan systems to highlight what they held in common, and to revitalize the practices that had connected ritual worship with the highly evolved philosophy of the time.

It is interesting to note the parallels between Iamblichus' world and the world of Thomas Anson. Both lived in a time of philosophical enlightenment, and in both cases the enlightenment of their times were negatively affecting aspects of the established religion in their environment.

For Iamblichus, the enlightenment of the Neoplatonist schools had effectively transformed the philosophies associated with pagan religious practice into an elitist system far removed from the common man. By contrast, the masses found the growing faith of Christianity much more accessible to them.

In Anson's world, the Age of Enlightenment had ushered in a different set of problems. The Thirty Years War had demonstrated the horrors of religious warfare throughout Europe. At the same time, the rise of humanism through the growing fields of science, politics and economics had begun to create an environment characterized by rationalism and materialism, which began to distance itself from all elements of supernatural belief. Faith-based belief systems from religion to mysticism and magic all found themselves more and more to be on the outside of the intellectual, and ultimately the cultural growth of western consciousness.

---

[29] M. Anis, "The First Egyptian Society in London (1741-1743)", *Bulletin De L'Institute Francais D'Archaeologie D'Orientale* (50) 1952, 103.

[30] England adopted the Gregorian calendar in 1752, but it had by then accumulated a difference of 11 days from the Julian Calendar, which had to be corrected. As a result, the solstice which would currently be celebrated on December 22 would have fallen on December 11 in 1742.

[31] M. Anis, 99.

[32] Rachel Finnegan, "The Divan Club, 1744-46", *EJOS*, IX (2006), No. 9, 3-4.

[33] M. Anis, 99.

[34] M. Anis, 103.

[35] Geoffrey Ashe, *The Hell-Fire Clubs, A History of Anti-Morality*, Rev.ed.. (Gloucestershire: Sutton Publishing Limited, 2000).

Closing Thoughts

THE MYSTERIES BEFORE US

To believe that Thomas Anson built a monument on his Arcadian-themed estate depicting a syncretic goddess figure takes no great stretch of the imagination. There are other works on the Estate that identify a special significance for a Queen of Heaven, such as the plasterwork ceiling depicting Apollo and the Hours, led by Aurora, the inclusion of a medallion in the ceiling portraying Isis, the statue of Leda and the Swan in the garden and the painting of the Immaculate

Figure 16: Painting of the Immaculate Conception, hanging in the Red Drawing Room at the Shugborough Estate. ©National Trust Images/John Hammond

Conception that still hangs in the Red Drawing Room. That Thomas Anson created the Shepherdess's Tomb with special care, honoring the traditional mystery schools of the west in the monument's design and execution, is also no surprise. When one considers that some of Anson's closest associates were members of Dashwood's Monks of Medmenham, who created underground chambers and held private rites honoring the Bona Dea, Anson's monument is a clear fit in the greater contemporary culture he lived in, though perhaps more attuned to his gentlemanly style.

To what extent the possible theurgic elements of the monument and its inscription were reflective of a personal belief system we may never know. They could have been artistic only, or perhaps they had their genesis in some selective group with a shared passion for such ideas. Or they could indicate a deep personal interest on the part of Thomas Anson, whether shared with others or not. I tend to believe that the connection with Thomas Anson was very real, if only for the description given to us by Thomas Pennant, that "he was wont often to hang over it in affectionate and firm meditation."[36]

The one question, perhaps, is why the choice of Mary Magdalen as Anson's Shepherdess? That may forever elude us. It seems evident that Thomas Anson saw her as a syncretic version of the goddess figure that included the Christian element. One might wonder why he did not choose the Virgin Mary, but that may have been too closely aligned with the Catholic Church for a man with an unorthodox set of beliefs and raised in a Protestant culture.

More likely, Thomas Anson was attracted towards Mary Magdalen as a modern type of the biblical Eve. This was not a new idea, as it had been introduced to Christian theology by Saint Hippolytus of Rome in the third century. Just as the pair of Adam and Eve represented the fall of man in the Garden of Eden, Jesus and Mary Magdalen became a spiritual pair representative of the redemption of man at the garden tomb on Easter morning.[37] Susan Haskins, in her examination of Hippolytus's approach to Mary Magdalen, writes:

> …Having found Christ in the garden, Mary Magdalen becomes the new Eve. As the old Eve had forfeited her right to the tree of life in the Garden of Eden, Mary Magdalen/Martha-Mary now cling passionately to Christ having found him, the Tree of Life, in the Easter garden where life rises anew…And here in Hippolytus is possibly the first appearance of the title which recognizes the importance of Mary Magdalen's…role in announcing the resurrection to the apostles: for bringing mankind hope of eternal life and for compensating for the first Eve's sin, the New Eve becomes "Apostle to the Apostles."[38]

There is also a possibility that Mary Magdalen's special place among members of various gnostic Christian sects might explain Anson's secret regard for her. However, the Gnostic gospels, which give us the strongest evidence of that tradition, were not discovered until after Thomas Anson's death. Most of the knowledge we have of Mary Magdalen's special regard as a spiritual leader, comes to us in manuscripts hidden in the deserts of Egypt and discovered almost two hundred years after Thomas Anson's passing, among the Nag Hammadi manuscripts.

Perhaps there was a secret tradition which Thomas Anson was initiated into that maintained her status as a spiritual leader. We know that gnostic ideas were transmitted throughout the middle ages and the renaissance in esoteric traditions such as alchemy and Kabbalah. And there were certainly many groups and individuals with an interest in exploring such areas of study. We may never know more, though, as the esoteric nature of such traditions leaves us very little in the manner of documented scholarship.

Another possibility is that Anson was exposed to an early gnostic text which had not officially been made public. Throughout the 18th Century there was a great deal of interest in recovering rare texts from the Far East, and many private collectors among Anson's friends and associates. When London physician and bibliophile Anthony Askew died less than a year after Thomas Anson, the Askew Codex was found in his library. This codex contained the first known Coptic translation of the *Pistis Sophia*, a gnostic gospel in which Mary Magdalen played a significant role as a spiritual leader.

Some of Anson's associates from the Egyptian Society were close with Anthony Askew,[39] so Anson may have been aware of private scholarship regarding this or other similar privately held works. What's more, Dr. Richard Mead, who was the Anson family physician, gave Dr. Askew his clientele when he became too old to practice medicine,[40] so Anthony Askew may have actually been Thomas Anson's doctor and had a direct personal relationship with him. Nevertheless, these possibilities are but blind conjecture.

The most plausible idea is that Thomas Anson, with a strong regard for syncretic philosophies, saw Mary Magdalen as a metaphorical figure, representative of the sacred feminine goddess from many cultures, united now in a Christianized form. We see her etched in marble, nobly standing above the sepulcher, calmly overseeing the disciple shepherds as they excitedly wonder at the tomb in the garden.

And perhaps in that scene we find the central theme of the whole Shugborough estate: an earthly form of the ideal Platonic garden, sharing aspects of all divine gardens from all cultures. We see it in the beauty of the landscape, the artwork representative of so many cultures, the interweaving of Eden and the Easter-morning garden, and perhaps one more place. As we close this study, we share one final image, which the Ansons commissioned for their family china.

This piece centers on a lone tree, standing in a garden surrounded by the many monuments of the Shugborough estate. The human forms have vanished, leaving their artifacts behind. But in the tree we see seven pieces of fruit hanging, next to a garland of roses.

Here we see the eclectic Shugborough estate depicted as a vision of Hesperides, the garden of Juno. The fruit (bread-fruit, in honor of those carried by George Anson on his voyage around the world) represent the golden apples which grew on the tree in the center of the garden,

Figure 17: China from the Shugborough collection. © National Trust Images/Andy Voke

guarded by the serpent Ladon. Indeed, the fruit are even arranged in a rough depiction of the constellation Ursa Minor, which is made up of the seven daughters of Atlas – the Hesperides. The rose garland represents Ladon, hanging from the branches of the tree, later transformed into the constellation Draco. For Thomas Anson, just as Mary Magdalen represented all forms of the feminine aspect of God, embodied in one woman here on earth, Shugborough represented all forms of the sacred garden, reflective of a greater, purer heavenly source, but tended by its keeper, Thomas Anson, here on earth.

In the end, even if we believe the decryption of the Shugborough inscription that I have suggested, there are still many mysteries left before us. We may never know exactly how or why Thomas Anson developed a special, sacred regard for Mary Magdalen. We may never know if the monument was purely a work of art or whether it held a mystical, theurgic purpose. But one thing is certain: the Shepherdess still maintains her grace and her mystery, whatever conjecture we may form about her nature. Thomas Anson never betrayed his secrets. Nevertheless, like the *sunthemata* of the ancient world, the Shepherdess stands like a lone clue, beckoning us to contemplate a better understanding of the truths that lay hidden in her silent memorial of stone.

---

[36] Pennant, *Journey*, 93.

[37] Susan Haskins, *Mary Magdalen: Myth and Metaphor*, (Old Saybrook: Konecky & Konecky, 1993), 58-67.

[38] Haskins, 65.

[39] A. E. Gunther, *The Life of the Rev. Thomas Birch D.D., F.R.S.*, (Suffolk: The Halesworth Press), 31-33.

[40] William MacMichael, *The Gold-headed Cane* (New York: Paul B. Hoeber, 1915).

APPENDIX A

Reverse Engineering the Possible Keys

Name								Key 1 Vigenère								Key 2 Sestri							
1	2	3	4	5	6	7	8	1	2	3	4	5	6	7	8	1	2	3	4	5	6	7	8
A	b	i	g	a	i	l	e	O	T	G	M	V	S	K	R	N	S	F	L	U	R	J	Q
A	b	i	g	a	i	l	l	O	T	G	M	V	S	K	K	N	S	F	L	U	R	J	J
A	d	d	e	l	i	n	e	O	R	L	O	K	S	I	R	N	Q	K	N	J	R	H	Q
A	d	d	e	n	e	l	l	O	R	L	O	I	W	K	K	N	Q	K	N	H	V	J	J
A	d	d	i	a	n	a	l	O	R	L	K	V	N	V	K	N	Q	K	J	U	M	U	J
A	d	d	i	l	i	n	a	O	R	L	K	K	S	I	V	N	Q	K	J	J	R	H	U
A	d	d	i	l	y	n	e	O	R	L	K	K	C	I	R	N	Q	K	J	J	B	H	Q
A	d	d	i	n	a	l	l	O	R	L	K	I	A	K	K	N	Q	K	J	H	Z	J	J
A	d	d	i	n	e	l	l	O	R	L	K	I	W	K	K	N	Q	K	J	H	V	J	J
A	d	e	r	l	i	n	e	O	R	K	B	K	S	I	R	N	Q	J	A	J	R	H	Q
A	l	e	s	a	b	e	t	O	J	K	A	V	Z	R	C	N	I	J	Z	U	Y	Q	B
A	l	e	s	o	n	n	e	O	J	K	A	H	N	I	R	N	I	J	Z	G	M	H	Q
A	l	i	c	e	s	o	n	O	J	G	Q	R	I	H	I	N	I	F	P	Q	H	G	H
A	l	i	s	o	n	n	e	O	J	G	A	H	N	I	R	N	I	F	Z	G	M	H	Q
A	l	l	e	n	s	o	n	O	J	D	O	I	I	H	I	N	I	C	N	H	H	G	H
A	l	l	e	s	o	n	n	O	J	D	O	D	M	I	I	N	I	C	N	C	L	H	H
A	l	l	i	c	i	e	n	O	J	D	K	T	S	R	I	N	I	C	J	S	R	Q	H
A	l	l	i	n	s	o	n	O	J	D	K	I	I	H	I	N	I	C	J	H	H	G	H
A	l	l	i	s	i	n	a	O	J	D	K	D	S	I	V	N	I	C	J	C	R	H	U
A	l	l	i	s	i	n	e	O	J	D	K	D	S	I	R	N	I	C	J	C	R	H	Q
A	l	l	i	s	o	n	e	O	J	D	K	D	M	I	R	N	I	C	J	C	L	H	Q
A	l	l	i	s	o	n	n	O	J	D	K	D	M	I	I	N	I	C	J	C	L	H	H
A	n	a	s	t	a	s	i	O	H	O	A	C	A	D	N	N	G	N	Z	B	Z	C	M
A	n	e	r	i	l	l	a	O	H	K	B	N	P	K	V	N	G	J	A	M	O	J	U
A	p	o	l	l	i	n	a	O	F	A	H	K	S	I	V	N	E	Z	G	J	R	H	U
A	p	p	o	l	i	n	a	O	F	Z	E	K	S	I	V	N	E	Y	D	J	R	H	U
A	p	p	o	l	l	i	n	O	F	Z	E	K	P	N	I	N	E	Y	D	J	O	M	H
A	r	a	b	a	e	l	l	O	D	O	R	V	W	K	K	N	C	N	Q	U	V	J	J
A	t	k	i	n	s	o	n	O	B	E	K	I	I	H	I	N	A	D	J	H	H	G	H
A	v	e	r	i	l	d	e	O	Z	K	B	N	P	S	R	N	Y	J	A	M	O	R	Q

Name								Key 1 Vigenère								Key 2 Sestri							
1	2	3	4	5	6	7	8	1	2	3	4	5	6	7	8	1	2	3	4	5	6	7	8
A	v	i	r	i	l	l	a	O	Z	G	B	N	P	K	V	N	Y	F	A	M	O	J	U
B	a	r	b	a	r	a	h	N	U	X	R	V	J	V	O	M	T	W	Q	U	I	U	N
B	a	r	b	a	r	a	y	N	U	X	R	V	J	V	X	M	T	W	Q	U	I	U	W
B	a	r	b	a	r	e	y	N	U	X	R	V	J	R	X	M	T	W	Q	U	I	Q	W
B	a	r	b	a	r	i	a	N	U	X	R	V	J	N	V	M	T	W	Q	U	I	M	U
B	a	r	b	a	r	i	e	N	U	X	R	V	J	N	R	M	T	W	Q	U	I	M	Q
B	a	r	b	a	r	r	y	N	U	X	R	V	J	E	X	M	T	W	Q	U	I	D	W
B	a	r	b	a	r	y	e	N	U	X	R	V	J	X	R	M	T	W	Q	U	I	W	Q
B	a	r	b	e	r	e	y	N	U	X	R	R	J	R	X	M	T	W	Q	Q	I	Q	W
B	a	r	b	e	r	i	e	N	U	X	R	R	J	N	R	M	T	W	Q	Q	I	M	Q
B	a	r	b	e	r	r	e	N	U	X	R	R	J	E	R	M	T	W	Q	Q	I	D	R
B	a	r	b	e	r	r	y	N	U	X	R	R	J	E	X	M	T	W	Q	Q	I	D	W
B	a	r	b	e	r	y	e	N	U	X	R	R	J	X	R	M	T	W	Q	Q	I	W	Q
B	a	t	h	s	h	e	b	N	U	V	L	D	T	R	U	M	T	U	K	C	S	Q	T
B	e	a	t	r	i	c	e	N	Q	O	Z	E	S	T	R	M	P	N	Y	D	R	S	Q
B	e	i	t	r	e	s	s	N	Q	G	Z	E	W	D	D	M	P	F	Y	D	V	C	C
B	e	r	b	a	r	i	e	N	Q	X	R	V	J	N	R	M	P	W	Q	U	I	M	Q
B	e	t	r	e	c	c	a	N	Q	V	B	R	Y	T	V	M	P	U	A	Q	X	S	U
B	e	t	t	e	i	r	e	N	Q	V	Z	R	S	E	R	M	P	U	Y	Q	R	D	Q
B	e	t	t	e	r	a	s	N	Q	V	Z	R	J	V	D	M	P	U	Y	Q	I	U	C
B	e	t	t	e	r	e	s	N	Q	V	Z	R	J	R	D	M	P	U	Y	Q	I	Q	C
B	e	t	t	i	r	e	i	N	Q	V	Z	N	J	R	N	M	P	U	Y	M	I	Q	M
B	e	t	t	r	e	s	s	N	Q	V	Z	E	W	D	D	M	P	U	Y	D	V	C	C
B	e	t	t	r	i	c	e	N	Q	V	Z	E	S	T	R	M	P	U	Y	D	R	S	Q
B	e	t	t	r	i	e	s	N	Q	V	Z	E	S	R	D	M	P	U	Y	D	R	Q	C
B	e	t	t	r	i	s	s	N	Q	V	Z	E	S	D	D	M	P	U	Y	D	R	C	C
B	i	l	l	h	a	g	h	N	M	D	H	O	A	P	O	M	L	C	G	N	Z	O	N
B	r	i	d	g	e	t	t	N	D	G	P	P	W	C	C	M	C	F	O	O	V	B	B
B	r	i	d	g	g	e	t	N	D	G	P	P	U	R	C	M	C	F	O	O	T	Q	B
B	r	i	d	g	i	t	t	N	D	G	P	P	S	C	C	M	C	F	O	O	R	B	B
B	r	i	d	j	e	t	t	N	D	G	P	M	W	C	C	M	C	F	O	L	V	B	B
C	a	n	c	i	l	l	a	M	U	B	Q	N	P	K	V	L	T	A	P	M	O	J	U
C	a	r	o	l	i	n	a	M	U	X	E	K	S	I	V	L	T	W	D	J	R	H	U
C	a	r	o	l	i	n	e	M	U	X	E	K	S	I	R	L	T	W	D	J	R	H	Q
C	a	s	a	n	d	r	a	M	U	W	S	I	X	E	V	L	T	V	R	H	W	D	U

Name								Key 1 Vigenère								Key 2 Sestri							
1	2	3	4	5	6	7	8	1	2	3	4	5	6	7	8	1	2	3	4	5	6	7	8
C	a	t	c	h	i	s	i	M	U	V	Q	O	S	D	N	L	T	U	P	N	R	C	M
C	a	t	e	a	r	a	n	M	U	V	O	V	J	V	I	L	T	U	N	U	I	U	H
C	a	t	e	r	i	a	n	M	U	V	O	E	S	V	I	L	T	U	N	D	R	U	H
C	a	t	e	r	i	n	e	M	U	V	O	E	S	I	R	L	T	U	N	D	R	H	Q
C	a	t	h	a	r	e	n	M	U	V	L	V	J	R	I	L	T	U	K	U	I	Q	H
C	a	t	h	a	r	i	n	M	U	V	L	V	J	N	I	L	T	U	K	U	I	M	H
C	a	t	h	e	r	a	i	M	U	V	L	R	J	V	N	L	T	U	K	Q	I	U	M
C	a	t	h	e	r	a	n	M	U	V	L	R	J	V	I	L	T	U	K	Q	I	U	H
C	a	t	h	e	r	e	n	M	U	V	L	R	J	R	I	L	T	U	K	Q	I	Q	H
C	a	t	h	e	r	i	n	M	U	V	L	R	J	N	I	L	T	U	K	Q	I	M	H
C	a	t	h	e	r	n	e	M	U	V	L	R	J	I	R	L	T	U	K	Q	I	H	Q
C	a	t	h	e	r	o	n	M	U	V	L	R	J	H	I	L	T	U	K	Q	I	G	H
C	a	t	h	e	r	y	e	M	U	V	L	R	J	X	R	L	T	U	K	Q	I	W	Q
C	a	t	h	e	r	y	n	M	U	V	L	R	J	X	I	L	T	U	K	Q	I	W	H
C	a	t	h	r	i	n	e	M	U	V	L	E	S	I	R	L	T	U	K	D	R	H	Q
C	a	t	t	e	r	y	n	M	U	V	Z	R	J	X	I	L	T	U	Y	Q	I	W	H
C	a	t	t	y	r	y	n	M	U	V	Z	X	J	X	I	L	T	U	Y	W	I	W	H
C	h	a	r	i	t	e	e	M	N	O	B	N	H	R	R	L	M	N	A	M	G	Q	Q
C	h	a	r	i	t	y	e	M	N	O	B	N	H	X	R	L	M	N	A	M	G	W	Q
C	h	a	r	l	o	t	t	M	N	O	B	K	M	C	C	L	M	N	A	J	L	B	B
C	h	a	r	l	t	o	n	M	N	O	B	K	H	H	I	L	M	N	A	J	G	G	H
C	h	a	t	a	r	i	n	M	N	O	Z	V	J	N	I	L	M	N	Y	U	I	M	H
C	h	a	t	h	e	r	i	M	N	O	Z	O	W	E	N	L	M	N	Y	N	V	D	M
C	h	o	n	s	t	a	n	M	N	A	F	D	H	V	I	L	M	Z	E	C	G	U	H
C	h	r	i	s	h	b	e	M	N	X	K	D	T	U	R	L	M	W	J	C	S	T	Q
C	h	r	i	s	i	a	n	M	N	X	K	D	S	V	I	L	M	W	J	C	R	U	H
C	h	r	i	s	t	e	b	M	N	X	K	D	H	R	U	L	M	W	J	C	G	Q	T
C	h	r	i	s	t	i	a	M	N	X	K	D	H	N	V	L	M	W	J	C	G	M	U
C	h	r	y	s	t	a	b	M	N	X	U	D	H	V	U	L	M	W	T	C	G	U	T
C	h	u	r	c	h	i	a	M	N	U	B	T	T	N	V	L	M	T	A	S	S	M	U
C	i	c	e	l	i	a	m	M	M	M	O	K	S	V	J	L	L	L	N	J	R	U	I
C	i	c	i	l	i	a	m	M	M	M	K	K	S	V	J	L	L	L	J	J	R	U	I
C	i	c	i	l	l	i	a	M	M	M	K	K	P	N	V	L	L	L	J	J	O	M	U
C	i	c	i	l	l	i	e	M	M	M	K	K	P	N	R	L	L	L	J	J	O	M	Q
C	i	r	s	t	a	b	e	M	M	X	A	C	A	U	R	L	L	W	Z	B	Z	T	Q

Name								Key 1 Vigenère								Key 2 Sestri							
1	2	3	4	5	6	7	8	1	2	3	4	5	6	7	8	1	2	3	4	5	6	7	8
C	i	s	s	e	l	e	y	M	M	W	A	R	P	R	X	L	L	V	Z	Q	O	Q	W
C	i	s	s	i	l	l	a	M	M	W	A	N	P	K	V	L	L	V	Z	M	O	J	U
C	l	a	r	i	n	d	a	M	J	O	B	N	N	S	V	L	I	N	A	M	M	R	U
C	o	n	s	t	a	n	c	M	G	B	A	C	A	I	T	L	F	A	Z	B	Z	H	S
C	o	r	n	e	l	i	a	M	G	X	F	R	P	N	V	L	F	W	E	Q	O	M	U
C	r	i	s	t	i	a	n	M	D	G	A	C	S	V	I	L	C	F	Z	B	R	U	H
C	r	i	s	t	i	b	e	M	D	G	A	C	S	U	R	L	C	F	Z	B	R	T	Q
C	r	i	s	t	o	b	e	M	D	G	A	C	M	U	R	L	C	F	Z	B	L	T	Q
C	r	y	s	t	a	b	e	M	D	Q	A	C	A	U	R	L	C	P	Z	B	Z	T	Q
C	r	y	s	t	y	b	e	M	D	Q	A	C	C	U	R	L	C	P	Z	B	B	T	Q
C	u	r	c	h	i	a	n	M	A	X	Q	O	S	V	I	L	Z	W	P	N	R	U	H
C	u	r	s	t	a	b	e	M	A	X	A	C	A	U	R	L	Z	W	Z	B	Z	T	Q
C	u	s	t	a	n	c	e	M	A	W	Z	V	N	T	R	L	Z	V	Y	U	M	S	Q
C	u	s	t	a	n	t	i	M	A	W	Z	V	N	C	N	L	Z	V	Y	U	M	B	M
D	o	n	n	e	t	t	e	L	G	B	F	R	H	C	R	K	F	A	E	Q	G	B	Q
D	o	r	a	t	h	e	a	L	G	X	S	C	T	R	V	K	F	W	R	B	S	Q	U
D	o	r	a	t	h	e	y	L	G	X	S	C	T	R	X	K	F	W	R	B	S	Q	W
D	o	r	a	t	h	i	e	L	G	X	S	C	T	N	R	K	F	W	R	B	S	M	Q
D	o	r	a	t	h	o	e	L	G	X	S	C	T	H	R	K	F	W	R	B	S	G	Q
D	o	r	a	t	h	y	e	L	G	X	S	C	T	X	R	K	F	W	R	B	S	W	Q
D	o	r	e	t	h	i	a	L	G	X	O	C	T	N	V	K	F	W	N	B	S	M	U
D	o	r	i	e	t	h	i	L	G	X	K	R	H	O	N	K	F	W	J	Q	G	N	M
D	o	r	i	t	h	e	a	L	G	X	K	C	T	R	V	K	F	W	J	B	S	Q	U
D	o	r	i	t	h	e	e	L	G	X	K	C	T	R	R	K	F	W	J	B	S	Q	Q
D	o	r	i	t	h	i	e	L	G	X	K	C	T	N	R	K	F	W	J	B	S	M	Q
D	o	r	i	t	h	y	e	L	G	X	K	C	T	X	R	K	F	W	J	B	S	W	Q
D	o	r	o	o	t	h	y	L	G	X	E	H	H	O	X	K	F	W	D	G	G	N	W
D	o	r	o	t	h	e	a	L	G	X	E	C	T	R	V	K	F	W	D	B	S	Q	U
D	o	r	o	t	h	e	e	L	G	X	E	C	T	R	R	K	F	W	D	B	S	Q	Q
D	o	r	o	t	h	i	e	L	G	X	E	C	T	N	R	K	F	W	D	B	S	M	Q
D	o	r	o	t	h	y	e	L	G	X	E	C	T	X	R	K	F	W	D	B	S	W	Q
D	o	r	r	a	t	h	y	L	G	X	B	V	H	O	X	K	F	W	A	U	G	N	W
D	o	r	r	i	t	e	e	L	G	X	B	N	H	R	R	K	F	W	A	M	G	Q	Q
D	o	r	r	i	t	h	i	L	G	X	B	N	H	O	N	K	F	W	A	M	G	N	M
D	o	r	r	i	t	h	y	L	G	X	B	N	H	O	X	K	F	W	A	M	G	N	W

Name								Key 1 Vigenère								Key 2 Sestri							
1	2	3	4	5	6	7	8	1	2	3	4	5	6	7	8	1	2	3	4	5	6	7	8
D	o	r	r	i	t	i	e	L	G	X	B	N	H	N	R	K	F	W	A	M	G	M	Q
D	o	r	r	i	t	y	e	L	G	X	B	N	H	X	R	K	F	W	A	M	G	W	Q
D	o	r	r	o	t	h	i	L	G	X	B	H	H	O	N	K	F	W	A	G	G	N	M
D	o	r	r	o	t	h	y	L	G	X	B	H	H	O	X	K	F	W	A	G	G	N	W
D	o	r	r	y	t	h	y	L	G	X	B	X	H	O	X	K	F	W	A	W	G	N	W
D	o	r	t	h	i	t	h	L	G	X	Z	O	S	C	O	K	F	W	Y	N	R	B	N
D	o	r	y	t	h	e	y	L	G	X	U	C	T	R	X	K	F	W	T	B	S	Q	W
D	o	r	y	t	h	i	e	L	G	X	U	C	T	N	R	K	F	W	T	B	S	M	Q
D	r	u	s	i	l	l	a	L	D	U	A	N	P	K	V	K	C	T	Z	M	O	J	U
D	u	l	c	i	b	e	l	L	A	D	Q	N	Z	R	K	K	Z	C	P	M	Y	Q	J
E	b	b	a	l	i	n	e	K	T	N	S	K	S	I	R	J	S	M	R	J	R	H	Q
E	l	a	s	a	b	a	t	K	J	O	A	V	Z	V	C	J	I	N	Z	U	Y	U	B
E	l	a	s	a	b	e	t	K	J	O	A	V	Z	R	C	J	I	N	Z	U	Y	Q	B
E	l	a	z	e	b	e	t	K	J	O	T	R	Z	R	C	J	I	N	S	Q	Y	Q	B
E	l	e	a	n	o	r	a	K	J	K	S	I	M	E	V	J	I	J	R	H	L	D	U
E	l	e	a	n	o	u	r	K	J	K	S	I	M	B	E	J	I	J	R	H	L	A	D
E	l	e	i	b	e	t	h	K	J	K	K	U	W	C	O	J	I	J	J	T	V	B	N
E	l	e	i	n	o	u	r	K	J	K	K	I	M	B	E	J	I	J	H	L	A	D
E	l	e	n	o	r	a	m	K	J	K	F	H	J	V	J	J	I	J	E	G	I	U	I
E	l	e	o	n	o	r	u	K	J	K	E	I	M	E	B	J	I	J	D	H	L	D	A
E	l	e	s	a	b	a	t	K	J	K	A	V	Z	V	C	J	I	J	Z	U	Y	U	B
E	l	e	s	a	b	e	t	K	J	K	A	V	Z	R	C	J	I	J	Z	U	Y	Q	B
E	l	e	s	b	e	t	h	K	J	K	A	U	W	C	O	J	I	J	Z	T	V	B	N
E	l	e	s	e	p	e	t	K	J	K	A	R	L	R	C	J	I	J	Z	Q	K	Q	B
E	l	e	z	b	a	t	h	K	J	K	T	U	A	C	O	J	I	J	S	T	Z	B	N
E	l	i	a	n	o	r	a	K	J	G	S	I	M	F	V	J	I	F	R	H	L	D	U
E	l	i	o	n	a	r	a	K	J	G	E	I	A	E	V	J	I	F	D	H	Z	D	U
E	l	i	o	n	e	r	e	K	J	G	E	I	W	E	R	J	I	F	D	H	V	D	Q
E	l	i	o	n	o	r	a	K	J	G	E	I	M	E	V	J	I	F	D	H	L	D	U
E	l	i	z	a	b	e	t	K	J	G	T	V	Z	R	C	J	I	F	S	U	Y	Q	B
E	l	l	a	b	e	t	h	K	J	D	S	U	W	C	O	J	I	C	R	T	V	B	N
E	l	l	e	a	n	o	r	K	J	D	O	V	N	H	E	J	I	C	N	U	M	G	D
E	l	l	e	b	e	t	h	K	J	D	O	U	W	C	O	J	I	C	N	T	V	B	N
E	l	l	e	n	n	a	r	K	J	D	O	I	N	V	E	J	I	C	N	H	M	U	D
E	l	l	e	n	n	e	r	K	J	D	O	I	N	R	E	J	I	C	N	H	M	Q	D

Name								Key 1 Vigenère								Key 2 Sestri							
1	2	3	4	5	6	7	8	1	2	3	4	5	6	7	8	1	2	3	4	5	6	7	8
E	l	l	e	n	o	r	a	K	J	D	O	I	M	E	V	J	I	C	N	H	L	D	U
E	l	l	e	n	o	r	e	K	J	D	O	I	M	E	R	J	I	C	N	H	L	D	Q
E	l	l	e	n	o	u	r	K	J	D	O	I	M	B	E	J	I	C	N	H	L	A	D
E	l	l	e	o	n	o	r	K	J	D	O	H	N	H	E	J	I	C	N	G	M	G	D
E	l	l	e	s	b	a	t	K	J	D	O	D	Z	V	C	J	I	C	N	C	Y	U	B
E	l	l	e	s	e	b	e	K	J	D	O	D	W	U	R	J	I	C	N	C	V	T	Q
E	l	l	i	n	n	e	r	K	J	D	K	I	N	R	E	J	I	C	J	H	M	Q	D
E	l	l	i	n	n	o	r	K	J	D	K	I	N	H	E	J	I	C	J	H	M	G	D
E	l	l	i	n	o	r	a	K	J	D	K	I	M	E	V	J	I	C	J	H	L	D	U
E	l	l	i	n	o	r	i	K	J	D	K	I	M	E	N	J	I	C	J	H	L	D	M
E	l	l	i	n	o	u	r	K	J	D	K	I	M	B	E	J	I	C	J	H	L	A	D
E	l	l	i	o	n	e	r	K	J	D	K	H	N	R	E	J	I	C	J	G	M	Q	D
E	l	l	i	s	a	b	e	K	J	D	K	D	A	U	R	J	I	C	J	C	Z	T	Q
E	l	l	i	s	b	e	t	K	J	D	K	D	Z	R	C	J	I	C	J	C	Y	Q	B
E	l	l	i	s	e	b	e	K	J	D	K	D	W	U	R	J	I	C	J	C	V	T	Q
E	l	l	i	s	o	n	e	K	J	D	K	D	M	I	R	J	I	C	J	C	L	H	Q
E	l	l	s	b	e	t	h	K	J	D	A	U	W	C	O	J	I	C	Z	T	V	B	N
E	l	l	s	e	b	e	y	K	J	D	A	R	Z	R	X	J	I	C	Z	Q	Y	Q	W
E	l	l	y	s	a	b	e	K	J	D	U	D	A	U	R	J	I	C	T	C	Z	T	Q
E	l	l	z	e	b	e	t	K	J	D	T	R	Z	R	C	J	I	C	S	Q	Y	Q	B
E	l	l	z	i	b	a	t	K	J	D	T	N	Z	V	C	J	I	C	S	M	Y	U	B
E	l	s	a	b	e	t	h	K	J	W	S	U	W	C	O	J	I	V	R	T	V	B	N
E	l	s	a	p	e	t	h	K	J	W	S	G	W	C	O	J	I	V	R	F	V	B	N
E	l	s	e	b	e	t	h	K	J	W	O	U	W	C	O	J	I	V	N	T	V	B	N
E	l	s	e	b	e	y	t	K	J	W	O	U	W	X	C	J	I	V	N	T	V	W	B
E	l	s	e	b	y	t	h	K	J	W	O	U	C	C	O	J	I	V	N	T	B	B	N
E	l	s	e	p	a	t	h	K	J	W	O	G	A	C	O	J	I	V	N	F	Z	B	N
E	l	s	e	p	e	t	h	K	J	W	O	G	W	C	O	J	I	V	N	F	V	B	N
E	l	s	o	p	e	t	h	K	J	W	E	G	W	C	O	J	I	V	D	F	V	B	N
E	l	y	s	a	b	e	t	K	J	Q	A	V	Z	R	C	J	I	P	Z	U	Y	Q	B
E	l	y	z	a	i	b	e	K	J	Q	T	V	S	U	R	J	I	P	S	U	R	T	Q
E	l	z	a	b	e	t	h	K	J	P	S	U	W	C	O	J	I	O	R	T	V	B	N
E	l	z	e	a	b	e	t	K	J	P	O	V	Z	R	C	J	I	O	N	U	Y	Q	B
E	l	z	e	b	e	t	h	K	J	P	O	U	W	C	O	J	I	O	N	T	V	B	N
E	m	m	e	r	s	o	n	K	I	C	O	E	I	H	I	J	H	B	N	D	H	G	H

Name								Key 1 Vigenère								Key 2 Sestri							
1	2	3	4	5	6	7	8	1	2	3	4	5	6	7	8	1	2	3	4	5	6	7	8
E	r	r	i	n	g	t	o	K	D	X	K	I	U	C	H	J	C	W	J	H	T	B	G
E	s	e	b	e	y	t	h	K	C	K	R	R	C	C	O	J	B	J	Q	Q	B	B	N
E	s	s	a	b	e	l	l	K	C	W	S	U	W	K	K	J	B	V	R	T	V	J	J
E	s	s	e	b	e	l	l	K	C	W	O	U	W	K	K	J	B	V	N	T	V	J	J
E	s	s	e	b	e	t	h	K	C	W	O	U	W	C	O	J	B	V	N	T	V	B	N
E	s	s	y	b	e	l	l	K	C	W	U	U	W	K	K	J	B	V	T	T	V	J	J
E	s	z	a	b	e	l	l	K	C	P	S	U	W	K	K	J	B	O	R	T	V	J	J
E	t	h	o	l	b	r	e	K	B	H	E	K	Z	E	R	J	A	G	D	J	Y	D	Q
E	u	p	h	e	m	i	a	K	A	Z	L	R	O	N	V	J	Z	Y	K	Q	N	M	U
E	z	i	a	b	e	l	l	K	V	G	S	U	W	K	K	J	U	F	R	T	V	J	J
E	z	s	e	b	e	l	l	K	V	W	O	U	W	K	K	J	U	V	N	T	V	J	J
F	a	r	b	r	i	c	k	J	U	X	R	E	S	T	L	I	T	W	Q	D	R	S	K
F	e	n	w	i	c	k	e	J	Q	B	W	N	Y	L	R	I	P	A	V	M	X	K	Q
F	e	r	d	i	n	a	n	J	Q	X	P	N	N	V	I	I	P	W	O	M	M	U	H
F	l	a	n	d	e	r	s	J	J	O	F	S	W	E	D	I	I	N	E	R	V	D	C
F	l	a	u	n	d	e	r	J	J	O	Y	I	X	R	E	I	I	N	X	H	W	Q	D
F	l	a	w	r	e	n	c	J	J	O	W	E	W	I	T	I	I	N	V	D	V	H	S
F	l	o	r	a	n	c	e	J	J	A	B	V	N	T	R	I	I	Z	A	U	M	S	Q
F	l	o	r	e	n	c	e	J	J	A	B	R	N	T	R	I	I	Z	A	Q	M	S	Q
F	r	a	n	c	e	s	e	J	D	O	F	T	W	D	R	I	C	N	E	S	V	C	Q
F	r	a	n	c	i	e	s	J	D	O	F	T	S	R	D	I	C	N	E	S	R	Q	C
F	r	a	n	c	i	s	a	J	D	O	F	T	S	D	V	I	C	N	E	S	R	C	U
F	r	a	n	c	i	s	e	J	D	O	F	T	S	D	R	I	C	N	E	S	R	C	Q
F	r	a	n	n	c	e	s	J	D	O	F	I	Y	R	D	I	C	N	E	H	X	Q	C
F	r	a	s	e	n	c	e	J	D	O	A	R	N	T	R	I	C	N	Z	Q	M	S	Q
F	r	a	u	n	c	e	s	J	D	O	Y	I	Y	R	D	I	C	N	X	H	X	Q	C
F	r	a	u	n	c	i	s	J	D	O	Y	I	Y	N	D	I	C	N	X	H	X	M	C
G	a	i	n	f	o	r	t	I	U	G	F	Q	M	E	C	H	T	F	E	P	L	D	B
G	a	r	t	e	r	e	d	I	U	X	Z	R	J	R	S	H	T	W	Y	Q	I	Q	R
G	a	r	t	h	a	i	n	I	U	X	Z	O	A	N	I	H	T	W	Y	N	Z	M	H
G	a	r	t	h	e	r	e	I	U	X	Z	O	W	E	R	H	T	W	Y	N	V	D	Q
G	a	r	t	r	e	t	t	I	U	X	Z	E	W	C	C	H	T	W	Y	D	V	B	B
G	a	r	t	r	u	d	e	I	U	X	Z	E	G	S	R	H	T	W	Y	D	F	R	Q
G	e	o	r	g	i	n	a	I	Q	A	B	P	S	I	V	H	P	Z	A	O	R	H	U
G	e	r	t	r	u	d	e	I	Q	X	Z	E	G	S	R	H	P	W	Y	D	F	R	Q

Name								Key 1 Vigenère								Key 2 Sestri							
1	2	3	4	5	6	7	8	1	2	3	4	5	6	7	8	1	2	3	4	5	6	7	8
H	a	r	t	b	u	r	n	H	U	X	Z	U	G	E	I	G	T	W	Y	T	F	D	H
H	e	l	e	a	n	o	r	H	Q	D	O	V	N	H	E	G	P	C	N	U	M	G	D
H	e	l	e	n	o	r	a	H	Q	D	O	I	M	E	V	G	P	C	N	H	L	D	U
H	e	l	l	e	n	o	r	H	Q	D	H	R	N	H	E	G	P	C	G	Q	M	G	D
H	e	l	l	i	n	e	r	H	Q	D	H	N	N	R	E	G	P	C	G	M	M	Q	D
H	e	l	l	i	n	o	r	H	Q	D	H	N	N	H	E	G	P	C	G	M	M	G	D
H	e	l	l	y	m	e	r	H	Q	D	H	X	O	R	E	G	P	C	G	W	N	Q	D
H	e	n	r	i	e	t	t	H	Q	B	B	N	W	C	C	G	P	A	A	M	V	B	B
H	o	w	t	h	e	a	m	H	G	S	Z	O	W	V	J	G	F	R	Y	N	V	U	I
H	u	t	c	h	i	n	s	H	A	V	Q	O	S	I	D	G	Z	U	P	N	R	H	C
I	l	s	a	b	e	t	h	G	J	W	S	U	W	C	O	F	I	V	R	T	V	B	N
I	s	a	a	b	e	l	l	G	C	O	S	U	W	K	K	F	B	N	R	T	V	J	J
I	s	a	b	e	l	l	a	G	C	O	R	R	P	K	V	F	B	N	Q	Q	O	J	U
I	s	a	e	b	e	l	l	G	C	O	O	U	W	K	K	F	B	N	N	T	V	J	J
I	s	s	a	b	e	l	l	G	C	W	S	U	W	K	K	F	B	V	R	T	V	J	J
I	s	s	a	b	i	l	l	G	C	W	S	U	S	K	K	F	B	V	R	T	R	J	J
I	s	s	e	b	e	l	l	G	C	W	O	U	W	K	K	F	B	V	N	T	V	J	J
I	s	s	o	b	e	l	l	G	C	W	E	U	W	K	K	F	B	V	D	T	V	J	J
I	s	z	a	b	e	l	l	G	C	P	S	U	W	K	K	F	B	O	R	T	V	J	J
I	s	z	e	b	e	l	l	G	C	P	O	U	W	K	K	F	B	O	N	T	V	J	J
J	a	n	n	e	t	t	e	F	U	B	F	R	H	C	R	E	T	A	E	Q	G	B	Q
J	e	l	l	i	a	n	n	F	Q	D	H	N	A	I	I	E	P	C	G	M	Z	H	H
J	e	n	n	e	t	t	a	F	Q	B	F	R	H	C	V	E	P	A	E	Q	G	B	U
J	e	n	n	i	f	e	r	F	Q	B	F	N	V	R	E	E	P	A	E	M	U	Q	D
J	e	n	n	i	t	t	e	F	Q	B	F	N	H	C	R	E	P	A	E	M	G	B	Q
J	e	n	n	y	t	t	e	F	Q	B	F	X	H	C	R	E	P	A	E	W	G	B	Q
J	o	h	a	n	n	a	m	F	G	H	S	I	N	V	J	E	F	G	R	H	M	U	I
K	a	t	e	r	i	n	a	E	U	V	O	E	S	I	V	D	T	U	N	D	R	H	U
K	a	t	e	r	y	n	e	E	U	V	O	E	C	I	R	D	T	U	N	D	B	H	Q
K	a	t	h	e	r	a	i	E	U	V	L	R	J	V	N	D	T	U	K	Q	I	U	M
K	a	t	h	e	r	a	n	E	U	V	L	R	J	V	I	D	T	U	K	Q	I	U	H
K	a	t	h	e	r	e	e	E	U	V	L	R	J	R	R	D	T	U	K	Q	I	Q	Q
K	a	t	h	e	r	e	n	E	U	V	L	R	J	R	I	D	T	U	K	Q	I	Q	H
K	a	t	h	e	r	i	a	E	U	V	L	R	J	N	V	D	T	U	K	Q	I	M	U
K	a	t	h	e	r	i	n	E	U	V	L	R	J	N	I	D	T	U	K	Q	I	M	H

Name								Key 1 Vigenère								Key 2 Sestri							
1	2	3	4	5	6	7	8	1	2	3	4	5	6	7	8	1	2	3	4	5	6	7	8
K	a	t	h	e	r	n	e	E	U	V	L	R	J	I	R	D	T	U	K	Q	I	H	Q
K	a	t	h	e	r	o	n	E	U	V	L	R	J	H	I	D	T	U	K	Q	I	G	H
K	a	t	h	e	r	y	n	E	U	V	L	R	J	X	I	D	T	U	K	Q	I	W	H
K	a	t	h	r	i	n	e	E	U	V	L	E	S	I	R	D	T	U	K	D	R	H	Q
K	a	t	r	r	y	n	g	E	U	V	B	E	C	I	P	D	T	U	A	D	B	H	O
K	a	t	t	e	r	i	n	E	U	V	Z	R	J	N	I	D	T	U	Y	Q	I	M	H
K	e	t	h	e	r	a	n	E	Q	V	L	R	J	V	I	D	P	U	K	Q	I	U	H
K	e	t	h	e	r	o	n	E	Q	V	L	R	J	H	I	D	P	U	K	Q	I	G	H
K	i	r	c	h	i	n	e	E	M	X	Q	O	S	I	R	D	L	W	P	N	R	H	Q
K	i	r	s	h	i	o	n	E	M	X	A	O	S	H	I	D	L	W	Z	N	R	G	H
K	i	r	s	t	e	b	e	E	M	X	A	C	W	U	R	D	L	W	Z	B	V	T	Q
K	y	r	c	h	y	n	e	E	W	X	Q	O	C	I	R	D	V	W	P	N	B	H	Q
M	a	d	g	l	y	n	e	C	U	L	M	K	C	I	R	B	T	K	L	J	B	H	Q
M	a	d	y	l	y	n	e	C	U	L	U	K	C	I	R	B	T	K	T	J	B	H	Q
M	a	g	a	l	e	n	e	C	U	I	S	K	W	I	R	B	T	H	R	J	V	H	Q
M	a	g	a	r	e	t	a	C	U	I	S	E	W	C	V	B	T	H	R	D	V	B	U
M	a	g	d	a	l	e	n	C	U	I	P	V	P	R	I	B	T	H	O	U	O	Q	H
M	a	g	d	a	l	l	e	C	U	I	P	V	P	K	R	B	T	H	O	U	O	J	Q
M	a	g	d	e	l	e	n	C	U	I	P	R	P	R	I	B	T	H	O	Q	O	Q	H
M	a	g	d	e	l	i	n	C	U	I	P	R	P	N	I	B	T	H	O	Q	O	M	H
M	a	g	d	e	l	l	a	C	U	I	P	R	P	K	V	B	T	H	O	Q	O	J	U
M	a	r	g	a	e	r	t	C	U	X	M	V	W	E	C	B	T	W	L	U	V	D	B
M	a	r	g	a	r	e	e	C	U	X	M	V	J	R	R	B	T	W	L	U	I	Q	Q
M	a	r	g	a	r	e	r	C	U	X	M	V	J	R	E	B	T	W	L	U	I	Q	D
M	a	r	g	a	r	e	t	C	U	X	M	V	J	R	C	B	T	W	L	U	I	Q	B
M	a	r	g	a	r	g	e	C	U	X	M	V	J	P	R	B	T	W	L	U	I	O	Q
M	a	r	g	a	r	i	e	C	U	X	M	V	J	N	R	B	T	W	L	U	I	M	Q
M	a	r	g	a	r	i	t	C	U	X	M	V	J	N	C	B	T	W	L	U	I	M	B
M	a	r	g	a	r	r	e	C	U	X	M	V	J	E	R	B	T	W	L	U	I	D	Q
M	a	r	g	a	r	t	a	C	U	X	M	V	J	C	V	B	T	W	L	U	I	B	U
M	a	r	g	a	r	t	t	C	U	X	M	V	J	C	C	B	T	W	L	U	I	B	B
M	a	r	g	e	a	r	e	C	U	X	M	R	A	E	R	B	T	W	L	Q	Z	D	Q
M	a	r	g	e	r	e	a	C	U	X	M	R	J	R	V	B	T	W	L	Q	I	Q	U
M	a	r	g	e	r	e	t	C	U	X	M	R	J	R	C	B	T	W	L	Q	I	Q	B
M	a	r	g	e	r	e	y	C	U	X	M	R	J	R	X	B	T	W	L	Q	I	Q	W

Name								Key 1 Vigenère								Key 2 Sestri							
1	2	3	4	5	6	7	8	1	2	3	4	5	6	7	8	1	2	3	4	5	6	7	8
M	a	r	g	e	r	i	a	C	U	X	M	R	J	N	V	B	T	W	L	Q	I	M	U
M	a	r	g	e	r	i	e	C	U	X	M	R	J	N	R	B	T	W	L	Q	I	M	Q
M	a	r	g	e	r	i	u	C	U	X	M	R	J	N	B	B	T	W	L	Q	I	M	A
M	a	r	g	e	r	r	e	C	U	X	M	R	J	E	R	B	T	W	L	Q	I	D	Q
M	a	r	g	e	r	y	e	C	U	X	M	R	J	X	R	B	T	W	L	Q	I	W	Q
M	a	r	g	o	r	i	e	C	U	X	M	H	J	N	R	B	T	W	L	G	I	M	Q
M	a	r	g	r	a	t	e	C	U	X	M	E	A	C	R	B	T	W	L	D	Z	B	Q
M	a	r	g	r	a	t	t	C	U	X	M	E	A	C	C	B	T	W	L	D	Z	B	B
M	a	r	g	r	e	a	t	C	U	X	M	E	W	V	C	B	T	W	L	D	V	U	B
M	a	r	g	r	e	e	t	C	U	X	M	E	W	R	C	B	T	W	L	D	V	Q	B
M	a	r	g	r	e	t	a	C	U	X	M	E	W	C	V	B	T	W	L	D	V	B	U
M	a	r	g	r	e	t	e	C	U	X	M	E	W	C	R	B	T	W	L	D	V	B	Q
M	a	r	g	r	e	t	t	C	U	X	M	E	W	C	C	B	T	W	L	D	V	B	B
M	a	r	g	r	i	t	t	C	U	X	M	E	S	C	C	B	T	W	L	D	R	B	B
M	a	r	g	y	r	i	a	C	U	X	M	X	J	N	V	B	T	W	L	W	I	M	U
M	a	r	i	a	n	i	a	C	U	X	K	V	N	N	V	B	T	W	J	U	M	M	U
M	a	r	i	a	n	n	e	C	U	X	K	V	N	I	R	B	T	W	J	U	M	H	Q
M	a	r	i	a	r	a	m	C	U	X	K	V	J	V	J	B	T	W	J	U	I	U	I
M	a	r	i	e	l	l	a	C	U	X	K	R	P	K	V	B	T	W	J	Q	O	J	U
M	a	r	i	e	r	i	a	C	U	X	K	R	J	N	V	B	T	W	J	Q	I	M	U
M	a	r	i	e	r	i	e	C	U	X	K	R	J	N	R	B	T	W	J	Q	I	M	Q
M	a	r	i	e	r	y	e	C	U	X	K	R	J	X	R	B	T	W	J	Q	I	W	Q
M	a	r	i	l	l	a	m	C	U	X	K	K	P	V	J	B	T	W	J	J	O	U	I
M	a	r	i	o	r	g	e	C	U	X	K	H	J	P	R	B	T	W	J	G	I	O	Q
M	a	r	i	o	r	y	e	C	U	X	K	H	J	X	R	B	T	W	J	G	I	W	Q
M	a	r	j	e	r	i	e	C	U	X	J	R	J	N	R	B	T	W	I	Q	I	M	Q
M	a	r	j	o	r	i	a	C	U	X	J	H	J	N	V	B	T	W	I	G	I	M	U
M	a	r	j	o	r	i	e	C	U	X	J	H	J	N	R	B	T	W	I	G	I	M	Q
M	a	u	d	e	l	a	n	C	U	U	P	R	P	V	I	B	T	T	O	Q	O	U	H
M	a	u	d	e	l	i	n	C	U	U	P	R	P	N	I	B	T	T	O	Q	O	M	H
M	a	u	d	l	a	n	d	C	U	U	P	K	A	I	S	B	T	T	O	J	Z	H	R
M	e	r	g	e	r	i	e	C	Q	X	M	R	J	N	R	B	P	W	L	Q	I	M	Q
M	e	r	i	a	r	e	t	C	Q	X	K	V	J	R	C	B	P	W	J	U	I	Q	B
M	e	r	r	i	a	l	l	C	Q	X	B	N	A	K	K	B	P	W	A	M	Z	J	J
M	i	l	d	r	e	d	a	C	M	D	P	E	W	S	V	B	L	C	O	D	V	R	U

Name								Key 1 Vigenère								Key 2 Sestri							
1	2	3	4	5	6	7	8	1	2	3	4	5	6	7	8	1	2	3	4	5	6	7	8
M	i	l	i	s	a	t	a	C	M	D	K	D	A	C	V	B	L	C	J	C	Z	B	U
M	i	r	r	i	a	l	l	C	M	X	B	N	A	K	K	B	L	W	A	M	Z	J	J
M	o	o	r	e	c	o	c	C	G	A	B	R	Y	H	T	B	F	Z	A	Q	X	G	S
M	u	r	r	i	a	l	l	C	A	X	B	N	A	K	K	B	Z	W	A	M	Z	J	J
M	y	r	i	l	l	a	m	C	W	X	K	K	P	V	J	B	V	W	J	J	O	U	I
N	e	v	i	l	s	o	n	B	Q	T	K	K	I	H	I	A	P	S	J	J	H	G	H
N	i	c	h	o	l	s	o	B	M	M	L	H	P	D	H	A	L	L	K	G	O	C	G
P	a	r	n	i	e	l	l	Z	U	X	F	N	W	K	K	Y	T	W	E	M	V	J	J
P	a	t	i	e	n	c	e	Z	U	V	K	R	N	T	R	Y	T	U	J	Q	M	S	Q
P	a	t	t	e	s	o	n	Z	U	V	Z	R	I	H	I	Y	T	U	Y	Q	H	G	H
P	e	n	e	l	o	p	e	Z	Q	B	O	K	M	G	R	Y	P	A	N	J	L	F	Q
P	e	r	e	g	r	i	n	Z	Q	X	O	P	J	N	I	Y	P	W	N	O	I	M	H
P	e	t	r	o	n	n	e	Z	Q	V	B	H	N	I	R	Y	P	U	A	G	M	H	Q
P	h	i	l	l	e	s	e	Z	N	G	H	K	W	D	R	Y	M	F	G	J	V	C	Q
P	h	i	l	l	i	c	e	Z	N	G	H	K	S	T	R	Y	M	F	G	J	R	S	Q
P	h	i	l	l	i	p	a	Z	N	G	H	K	S	G	V	Y	M	F	G	J	R	F	U
P	h	i	l	l	i	p	p	Z	N	G	H	K	S	G	G	Y	M	F	G	J	R	F	F
P	h	i	l	l	i	s	e	Z	N	G	H	K	S	D	R	Y	M	F	G	J	R	C	Q
P	h	i	l	l	i	s	s	Z	N	G	H	K	S	D	D	Y	M	F	G	J	R	C	C
P	h	i	l	o	p	e	n	Z	N	G	H	H	L	R	I	Y	M	F	G	G	K	Q	H
P	h	i	l	o	t	i	s	Z	N	G	H	H	H	N	D	Y	M	F	G	G	G	M	C
P	i	c	k	e	r	i	n	Z	M	M	I	R	J	N	I	Y	L	L	H	Q	I	M	H
P	r	i	c	i	l	l	a	Z	D	G	Q	N	P	K	V	Y	C	F	P	M	O	J	U
P	r	i	s	c	i	l	l	Z	D	G	A	T	S	K	K	Y	C	F	Z	S	R	J	J
P	r	u	d	a	n	c	e	Z	D	U	P	V	N	T	R	Y	C	T	O	U	M	S	Q
P	r	u	d	o	n	c	e	Z	D	U	P	R	N	T	R	Y	C	T	O	Q	M	S	Q
R	a	c	h	a	e	l	l	X	U	M	L	V	W	K	K	W	T	L	K	U	V	J	J
R	a	t	c	h	e	l	l	X	U	V	Q	O	W	K	K	W	T	U	P	N	V	J	J
R	e	b	b	e	c	c	a	X	Q	N	R	R	Y	T	V	W	P	M	Q	Q	X	S	U
R	e	b	e	c	c	a	h	X	Q	N	O	T	Y	V	O	W	P	M	N	S	X	U	N
R	e	b	e	c	c	a	m	X	Q	N	O	T	Y	V	J	W	P	M	N	S	X	U	I
R	e	b	e	c	c	h	a	X	Q	N	O	T	Y	O	V	W	P	M	N	S	X	N	U
R	e	b	e	c	k	a	h	X	Q	N	O	T	Q	V	O	W	P	M	N	S	P	U	N
R	e	b	e	c	k	a	y	X	Q	N	O	T	Q	V	X	W	P	M	N	S	P	U	W
R	e	b	e	c	k	e	y	X	Q	N	O	T	Q	R	X	W	P	M	N	S	P	Q	W

Name								Key 1 Vigenère								Key 2 Sestri							
1	2	3	4	5	6	7	8	1	2	3	4	5	6	7	8	1	2	3	4	5	6	7	8
R	e	e	d	h	e	a	d	X	Q	K	P	O	W	V	S	W	P	J	O	N	V	U	R
R	h	e	b	e	c	c	a	X	N	K	R	R	Y	T	V	W	M	J	Q	Q	X	S	U
R	o	s	a	m	o	n	d	X	G	W	S	J	M	I	S	W	F	V	R	I	L	H	R
R	o	s	a	m	u	n	d	X	G	W	S	J	G	I	S	W	F	V	R	I	F	H	R
R	o	s	a	n	n	a	h	X	G	W	S	I	N	V	O	W	F	V	R	H	M	U	N
R	o	t	h	e	r	f	o	X	G	V	L	R	J	Q	H	W	F	U	K	Q	I	P	G
R	u	d	e	r	f	o	r	X	Λ	L	O	E	V	II	E	W	Z	K	N	D	U	G	D
S	e	s	s	i	l	a	y	W	Q	W	A	N	P	V	X	V	P	V	Z	M	O	U	W
S	i	n	g	l	e	t	o	W	M	B	M	K	W	C	H	V	L	A	L	J	V	B	G
S	i	s	s	e	l	i	e	W	M	W	A	R	P	N	R	V	L	V	Z	Q	O	M	Q
S	i	s	s	i	l	l	e	W	M	W	A	N	P	K	R	V	L	V	Z	M	O	J	Q
S	o	w	l	e	s	b	y	W	G	S	H	R	I	U	X	V	F	R	G	Q	H	T	W
S	u	s	a	n	a	y	e	W	A	W	S	I	A	X	R	V	Z	V	R	H	Z	W	Q
S	u	s	a	n	n	a	h	W	A	W	S	I	N	V	O	V	Z	V	R	H	M	U	N
S	u	s	a	n	n	a	y	W	A	W	S	I	N	V	X	V	Z	V	R	H	M	U	W
S	w	i	n	b	u	r	n	W	Y	G	F	U	G	E	I	V	X	F	E	T	F	D	H
S	y	s	s	e	l	l	y	W	W	W	A	R	P	K	X	V	V	V	Z	Q	O	J	W
T	h	a	y	m	a	z	i	V	N	O	U	J	A	W	N	U	M	N	T	I	Z	V	M
T	h	e	o	p	h	i	l	V	N	K	E	G	T	N	K	U	M	J	D	F	S	M	J
T	h	o	m	a	s	i	n	V	N	A	G	V	I	N	I	U	M	Z	F	U	H	M	H
T	h	o	m	a	s	o	n	V	N	A	G	V	I	H	I	U	M	Z	F	U	H	G	H
T	h	o	m	a	s	s	o	V	N	A	G	V	I	D	H	U	M	Z	F	U	H	C	G
T	h	o	m	a	z	e	n	V	N	A	G	V	B	R	I	U	M	Z	F	U	A	Q	H
T	h	o	m	a	z	i	n	V	N	A	G	V	B	N	I	U	M	Z	F	U	A	M	H
T	h	o	m	i	s	o	n	V	N	A	G	N	I	H	I	U	M	Z	F	M	H	G	H
T	h	o	m	l	i	n	s	V	N	A	G	K	S	I	D	U	M	Z	F	J	R	H	C
T	h	o	m	p	s	o	n	V	N	A	G	G	I	H	I	U	M	Z	F	F	H	G	H
T	h	o	m	y	s	o	n	V	N	A	G	X	I	H	I	U	M	Z	F	W	H	G	H
T	i	m	o	t	h	e	a	V	M	C	E	C	T	R	V	U	L	B	D	B	S	Q	U
T	o	m	i	s	i	n	e	V	G	C	K	D	S	I	R	U	F	B	J	C	R	H	Q
T	o	m	m	o	n	s	o	V	G	C	G	H	N	D	H	U	F	B	F	G	M	C	G
T	o	m	m	o	s	o	n	V	G	C	G	H	I	H	I	U	F	B	F	G	H	G	H
T	o	m	o	n	s	o	n	V	G	C	E	I	I	H	I	U	F	B	D	H	H	G	H
T	o	m	y	s	y	n	e	V	G	C	U	D	C	I	R	U	F	B	T	C	B	H	Q
T	r	a	p	h	o	e	n	V	D	O	D	O	M	R	I	U	C	N	C	N	L	Q	H

Name								Key 1 Vigenère								Key 2 Sestri							
1	2	3	4	5	6	7	8	1	2	3	4	5	6	7	8	1	2	3	4	5	6	7	8
T	r	i	p	h	e	n	a	V	D	G	D	O	W	I	V	U	C	F	C	N	V	H	U
T	r	y	p	h	e	n	a	V	D	Q	D	O	W	I	V	U	C	P	C	N	V	H	U
U	e	m	f	r	e	d	e	U	Q	C	N	E	W	S	R	T	P	B	M	D	V	R	Q
U	l	l	i	s	i	b	e	U	J	D	K	D	S	U	R	T	I	C	J	C	R	T	Q
U	r	s	e	l	l	a	y	U	D	W	O	K	P	V	X	T	C	V	N	J	O	U	W
U	r	s	i	l	l	a	y	U	D	W	K	K	P	V	X	T	C	V	J	J	O	U	W
U	r	s	i	l	l	e	y	U	D	W	K	K	P	R	X	T	C	V	J	J	O	Q	W
U	s	s	i	l	l	i	e	U	C	W	K	K	P	N	R	T	B	V	J	J	O	M	Q
V	i	o	l	e	t	t	a	T	M	A	H	R	H	C	V	S	L	Z	G	Q	G	B	U
W	a	s	e	t	e	l	l	S	U	W	O	C	W	K	K	R	T	V	N	B	V	J	J
W	e	n	e	f	r	i	d	S	Q	B	O	Q	J	N	S	R	P	A	N	P	I	M	R
W	i	n	i	f	r	e	d	S	M	B	K	Q	J	R	S	R	L	A	J	P	I	Q	R
W	i	n	i	f	r	i	d	S	M	B	K	Q	J	N	S	R	L	A	J	P	I	M	R
W	y	n	e	f	r	y	d	S	W	B	O	Q	J	X	S	R	V	A	N	P	I	W	R
W	y	n	i	f	f	r	y	S	W	B	K	Q	V	E	X	R	V	A	J	P	U	D	W
X	r	o	t	a	b	e	l	R	D	A	Z	V	Z	R	K	Q	C	Z	Y	U	Y	Q	J
Y	s	s	a	b	e	l	l	Q	C	W	S	U	W	K	K	P	B	V	R	T	V	J	J

About the Author

About the Author

Dave Ramsden has been captivated by history, mysteries and patterns ever since he was a child. He earned a Bachelor of Arts in History from Bridgewater State University and is a member of *Phi Alpha Theta*, an American honor society for Historians. Dave holds a Master of Arts in English from BSU and is also a member of American Mensa. He is currently the Chief Strategy Officer at Atrion Networking Corporation, and as such speaks and publishes regularly on business strategy, competitive intelligence and increasing the strategic value of IT within organizations.

Proud to be an Aspergian, Dave is active in raising Autism awareness both within and outside of the technology community and has spoken publicly on living with Autism Spectrum Disorder (ASD). He lives with his wife and family just outside of Boston, Massachusetts.

Index

INDEX

gnostic text 88

Great Work, The 39

Greek revival 15

• H •

Harpocrates 67

Hebrew Psalms 50

Hekate 34, 76

Hellfire Club 67, 78

Herod's Temple 35

humanism 77, 80

• I •

Iamblichus 70, 72, 78, 79, 80

Immaculate Conception 85

invocation formula 50, 51, 72

Isis 33, 34, 35, 46, 51, 54, 62, 63, 66, 76, 85

• J •

Jones, William (Sr.) 14, 70

Jupiter 33

• K •

Kabbalah 35, 37, 66, 70, 87

Kabbalistic 50, 55, 66, 72, 78

Kahn, David 7, 8

Kircher, Athanasius ix, 7, 50, 56, 62, 69, 70, 71, 72

• L •

Lady Psalter 53

Leda and the Swan 85

Les bergers d'Arcadie 16

letter frequency analysis 43

Lucius 34

Lykosoura 36

• M •

Macclesfield 14

1st Earl of Macclesfield, Thomas Parker 14, 38

Madame d'Urfé 37, 38, 39, 40, 41, 42

MAGDALEN 47, 51, 59

Magdalen, Mary 51, 52, 73, 86, 87, 88, 90

magic 8, 9, 38, 39, 81

magnum opus 38

Manes 28

Marian devotion 53

Marquise d'Urfé, Jeanne 38

Martinism 78

materialism 80

Mead, Dr. Richard 14, 88

Medmenham Abbey 67

Medmenham, Monks of 67, 86

Metamorphosis, The 33, 46

mother-goddess 33

mystery schools 33, 36, 60, 62, 64, 65, 66, 67, 76, 79, 86

Dionysian 66

Egyptian 66

Eleusinian 66

Made in the USA
San Bernardino, CA
16 April 2015